What people are saying about *Inspire, Persuade, Lead:*

"The concepts in *Inspire, Persuade, Lead* are incredibly powerful. It's guaranteed to facilitate growth. I put it on my "must read" list—not just for executives, but the entire organization."

> —Dan Mallin, chief operating officer,
> connect@jwt, a J Walter Thompson Company

"Today more than ever, the communication skills of leaders can determine mediocre successes from the grand-slam home runs. Paul's ability to package his insights into bite size pieces and provide REAL examples makes it easy to put in practice immediately regardless of your style. It's guaranteed to improve your effectiveness 10-fold."

> —Nancy Dahl, senior vice president of sales and
> marketing, Lifetouch Portrait Studios

"This book is one of the most practical books on communicating effectively that I've ever read. If people had a bite of their Humble Sandwich every now and then, and practiced only three or four of the Ten Commandments, their success at influencing others would skyrocket."

> —Robert C. Barnett, PhD, LP, executive
> vice president, MDA Leadership Consulting

"Paul's leadership programs have changed the way our teams think about communication—and leadership. This book will be a daily reference guide for every one of us."

> —Tim Schmitt, managing partner, Thrivent
> Financial for Lutherans, Minneapolis

"Knowing Paul, I've always assumed that his magic—making anyone who works with him feel valued, respected and energized—had to be innate. Here, he reveals it is a behavior he has learned. This book is a gift—a trove of great stories crystallized into Paul's Ten Commandments and other put-it-to-work leadership lessons. It's a weekend read and a lifetime reference."
—Bob Brin, vice president, Padilla Speer Beardsley, Minneapolis

"Paul has a gift for crystallizing what it means to truly be a people-centered leader. His vivid stories, memorable props and clear pictures, paired with personal dynamism and enthusiasm, are contagious and transforming."
—Marilyn Sharpe, chief administrative officer, Youth & Family Institute of Augsburg College, Minneapolis

"*Inspire, Persuade, Lead* is a back-to-the-basics book with new and refreshing insight into the skills required today for leading and communicating. I highly recommend all levels of managers and leaders read this book and use the practical advice."
—Bob Jungbluth, president, Viracon Curvlite

"*Inspire, Persuade, Lead* provides leadership advice like you've never heard before! You can apply these strategies today and start to see immediate results!"
—Jim Gorman, media analyst, Prudential Securities, New York

INSPIRE
PERSUADE
LEAD

Communication Secrets of Excellent Leaders

Paul H. Batz

Beaver's Pond Press, Inc.
Edina,   Minnesota

ISBN 1-931646-24-4

Library of Congress Catalog Number: 2001096146

Printed in the United States of America.

First Printing: September 2001
Second Printing: May 2004
Third Printing: September 2008

08 07 06 05 04   6 5 4 3 2

Beaver's Pond Press, Inc.

5125 Danen's Drive
Edina, MN 55439-1465
(952) 829-8818
www.beaverspondpress.com

Without
great leadership,
nothing works.™

a publication of MDA Leadership Consulting,
Minneapolis, Minnesota, 2008

Contents

Commandment #7: Put It on Paper. 101

Commandment #8: Be Careful What You Call Things 113

Commandment #9: Let Your Enthusiasm Light the Fire 127

Foreword

EVERY ONCE IN AWHILE I THINK, "HOW IN THE WORLD DID I GET TO BE THE CEO OF SUCH A GREAT ORGANIZATION—ALLIANZ LIFE INSURANCE COMPANY—SO FAST?" I started as a "numbers guy" with a B.A. in Accounting and licensure as a Certified Public Accountant, Chartered Financial Analyst, and securities broker. However, I received my *real* education through the business world—first at a Big Six firm, and then at Life USA as Treasurer at age 25 and CFO at the ripe age of 29. It's been quite a ride! Deep down, I really love finance, but I've learned through my finance responsibilities on the road to CEO that the numbers aren't the answer: it's really all about people.

Now, at Allianz Life, we're on a mission to sustain excellence and create healthy growth of everyone involved. We're focusing heavily on leading with values. The leadership challenge is to connect those values to everyday behaviors in our people so we can deliver the bottom-line results we all expect. We absolutely must inspire confidence at all levels of the organization and persuade people to stretch themselves and lead people with a keen sense of what's most important. If we don't, we'll fail.

I first met Paul Batz in 1995 through the Minneapolis City of Lakes Rotary Club. We are friends and leadership colleagues in our dedication to building a better community. *Inspire, Persuade, Lead:*

Communication Secrets of Excellent Leaders is a great, easy read. And, more importantly, it's a useful tool to help leaders be their best. It is full of simple, familiar principles and techniques that we should all know and do—but sometimes forget. Paul's message, *if people don't understand you, it's your problem,* is a simple reminder that our job as leaders is never done. I believe leaders today need to understand our audience and communicate in their language, not ours. If that means a "numbers guy" has to learn to communicate with stories and lead with questions, then I'll do it to be more effective.

Today, I lead as if our financial success is an *outcome.* If we stay focused on value-driven leadership—challenging, supporting, and holding people accountable—we will be very successful. That means we need to inspire, persuade and lead. It isn't easy, but it's very rewarding.

Happy reading.

Mark Zesbaugh
CEO, Allianz Life
2004

Acknowledgments

I ADMIRE ANYONE WHO HAS EVER PUT THEMSELVES ON THE LINE TO RUN A MARATHON OR WRITE A BOOK. We all know that introspection is the greatest test. The reward for finishing is a victory that lasts a lifetime. Of course you'd like to thank everyone who encouraged you along the way . . .

Now with our second edition of *Inspire, Persuade, Lead* it's *even more important* to say thanks to every one of you who shared your experiences, especially those recorded here.

Thanks to my friends at MDA, PSB, LSS and DLLC.

Thanks to Loren, Pete, Sean, Tim, Bob, Mark, Nancy, Peter, Joe, Scott and Sandra.

Thanks to the world's best family who makes me humble and whole.

And of course, Melinda, Kelly, and Shelly . . . I'll be darned—we did it.

Leaders Beware: If People Don't Understand You, It's *Your* Problem

"The more elaborate our means of communication, *the less we actually communicate.*"
—Joseph Priestley, English Scientist and Theologian, 1733-1804

"*I JUST LOVE WORKING FOR DICK KOVACEVICH,*" said Larry Haeg, executive vice president for Wells Fargo & Company, as we talked over lunch one bright winter afternoon when Larry was back in Minnesota. He was emphatic as he continued:

> He's a terrific leader. I admire him for so many reasons, but mainly because he is twice the communicator of you and me put together. After all I've seen in this job, I really do believe the best leaders are the best communicators. Dick knows how to inspire people to be their very best—to work toward the right goals and to make organizations like Wells Fargo successful for the long haul.

As CEO of Wells Fargo & Company, Dick Kovacevich is one of the most celebrated business leaders of the decade. It's obvious when listening to Larry that he is engaged with his leader and committed to the long-term success of Wells Fargo & Company. When was the last time you heard someone say with unbridled enthusiasm: I just *love* working for my leader?

It was refreshing to sit and listen to Larry describe what it's like working for Dick. More often, people report the opposite. They freely offer frustrations about leaders who approach their world from an action list—marking off "must do today" items, then quickly moving on to the next item on the list. They are smart, talented people but not excellent leaders.

I've known Larry for a long time and we've enjoyed many good conversations, but that particular conversation sparked my interest in communication as a fundamental leadership tool, one largely ignored in MBA curriculum and other leadership development programs. For me, it crystallized 15 years of communication experience into a single concept—*the best leaders are the best communicators.* It was one of those "ah-ha" moments and the concept became the framework for my popular *Ten Commandments of Leadership Communication* workshop, and the motivation for *Inspire, Persuade, Lead.*

So, what do you think Dick Kovacevich had to say to Larry Haeg's glowing endorsement of him as a communicator? Dick shared these thoughts with me when I had a chance to sit down with him after the Norwest/Wells Fargo merger was completed.

You know, I don't come to work every day saying, "I'm going to be a great communicator today." I'm simply here to help the businesses succeed. They're not there to help me succeed! If they're all succeeding, I'll be very, very successful. It's obvious that communication plays a great part in the equation. It's my job. I'm really not inclined to even think of myself as a communicator—I'm an engineer. If I'm good at all, it's with a lot of practice. It doesn't come naturally. It's just not something I attribute to myself. But I do know one thing: Communication is a broader subject than most people think. It's not just being a great speaker like Ronald Reagan or Winston Churchill. It's doing the little things to make sure you are understood.

He went on to share an example.

Like during the Norwest/Wells Fargo merger, we had to keep it all secret for obvious reasons. But when the deal was finally done, we agreed that we could make a big difference, with very little effort, by leaving group phone messages. So, at five o'clock in the morning, I was up leaving messages for people all across the country. That doesn't have anything to do with making great speeches. It's doing whatever it takes in influencing a group of people to do their job better—or think better— of Wells Fargo than they would have if they hadn't heard our message.

The War is Waging

The explosion of communication technology fueled by the Internet has created unprecedented opportunity. Not since Johann Gutenberg and Alexander Graham Bell has there been such a revolution. But this new culture of bits and bytes, real time, and virtual reality has created its own crisis. Computers on every desk, fiber optics, and wireless wonders have people more connected than ever before. But it's definitely making life more complicated. As Joseph Priestley reminds us, in the era of "communication," we seem to be sliding backwards in our ability to communicate.

Most people find themselves getting stuck in the crossfire of a sophisticated battle for our attention. Everywhere we turn, a clever trick tries to capture our mind. Marketers have decided they value our attention so much, they'll settle for just one split second—several hundred times a day. It's easy to understand why most people believe attention spans are shrinking. Marketing expert and author Al Ries agrees: "Today, communication itself is the problem," he writes in his book *Positioning: The Battle for Your Mind* (McGraw Hill, 1981). "We have become the world's first over-communicated society. Each year, we send more and receive less." Just keeping up with all this information is turning even the most effervescent extroverts into closet introverts—people trying desperately to keep up with overwhelming amounts of e-mail, voicemail, snail mail, and the plethora of newspapers, newsletters, trade journals, and magazines considered required reading.

This creates a new reality for leaders. Today, we need to fight the urge to be information-centered, and force ourselves to be people-centered. Information doesn't execute the strategic plan—people do. The bottom line for leadership today is this: **If people don't understand you, it's *your* problem**—not theirs. For some leaders, this is a heavy burden; a new behavior. It means they need to be clear in their own mind about what they are trying to accomplish. It also means they need to understand the people important to their success.

As Kovacevich said, it's hard work. Today there is more competition for attention than ever before. How do you really know if the people important to your success understand your message? You need to ask. You have to circle back time and time again, checking and rechecking to make certain they understand. That's the cornerstone of people who inspire, persuade, and lead today.

People Communicate, Not Organizations

Take a second and reflect on your personal experience.

- Who is the best leader you've encountered?
- Was that person open or closed with information?
- Did that person paint a clear picture of success or keep you in the dark?
- Did that person build your confidence or tear you down?
- Did you clearly understand your role?

If you haven't experienced excellent leadership, you've probably worked with at least one poor leader. What, specifically, did you learn *not to do*?

With Larry's endorsement reinforcing my own intuition, I started to interpret other expert findings that added credibility to my belief that the foundation for excellent leadership is this—*the best leaders are the best communicators*. Two highly respected organizations, Walker Information and the Hudson Institute, jointly executed the 1999 National Employee Benchmark Study on Employee Commitment in the Workplace. They found that employees are looking for a workplace that above all else has *care and concern for them as individuals*, and *is ethical and fair in its everyday business practices*.

The one common denominator of these two corporate qualities is *communication*. The employees who felt communication from leadership was poor did not rate their organization well on these two critical factors. But it's important to note that *organizations* don't communicate. *People* communicate—individuals like you and me make decisions every hour of every day whether to share information. And, it's not just the CEO and senior management; it is individuals at all levels within an organization—from administrators to middle management, nonprofits and corporations alike.

Perhaps even more powerful is the basic information uncovered by the Gallup organization. Armed with decades of experience in surveying employees, they honed their approach into 12 simple questions, called the G12. In the book, *First, Break All The Rules: What The World's Greatest Managers Do Differently*, Marcus Buckingham and Curt Coffman discuss many things related to organizational leadership. All of their work can be boiled down to this simple quote:

People join companies and leave managers.

At the very minimum, this underscores the high expectations held by the people important to your success. They want your support and attention. They want to be treated as individuals. They want to understand the big picture. They want to have clear direction about their roles. The good news is this: They will dedicate themselves to your vision if you are open with information, listen to them, treat them with respect, fill them with confidence, and give them the tools to succeed. If you don't, they will abandon you in a heartbeat.

General Norman Schwarzkopf agrees. During a speech to the annual Center for the American Experiment dinner in May 2001, he pointed to the need for exceptional communication skills in leading people.

Even in the strict regimen of the military, we need to constantly remind ourselves that we are not in the technology business, we are in the people business. You can stand there and shout at a $100-million plane "fly!" But planes don't fly unless people fly them. You can shout "drive" to a $100-million tank, but tanks don't drive unless people drive them. All the high technology in the world won't keep our world safe unless the people in the armed forces are aligned with our mission and are persuaded to engage in behaviors that are against their human nature. The people in Desert Storm put their lives on the line because they knew the leaders in my command cared about them. We constantly communicated to the soldiers that we valued them as patriots, as people who were important to their families, and as individuals.

The Ten Commandments

Studying famous leaders like Schwarzkopf—and not so famous leaders like the principal of my kids' elementary school—has been my lifelong habit. Watching, listening, analyzing. Simply asking myself questions: *"How do they do what they do? Why are they different? What specifically makes them excellent leaders? How do they inspire, persuade, and lead the people important to their success?"* I've learned there are some basic, fundamental communication principles that anyone can apply, which will help them become better leaders.

To simplify these communication principles and make them easier to remember I borrowed from the most widely read book in the Western world. Just as *The Ten Commandments* helped organize, or "package" a pathway to Judeo-Christian living, the *Ten Commandments of Leadership Communication* are intended to be a foundation for excellent leadership.

The commandments are:

- Commandment #1: Know yourself
- Commandment #2: Understand your audience
- Commandment #3: Disarm upfront
- Commandment #4: Tell stories
- Commandment #5: Be visual
- Commandment #6: Practice no surprises
- Commandment #7: Put it on paper
- Commandment #8: Be careful what you call things
- Commandment #9: Let your enthusiasm light the fire
- Commandment #10: Don't get defensive

The 11th Concept:
Repeat, Repeat, Repeat

Of course, since this is the second edition of this book, consultant creep has wiggled its way into an otherwise successful model. Upon reading the first published copy, a mentor of mine said "well done...except for one thing. You forgot to talk about the power of repetition." He was right. And since that day we've spoken about the power of repetition in every speech, every coaching session, and every leadership development program. The 11th "bonus" concept is simply called Repeat, Repeat, Repeat.

The Ten Commandments and bonus concept are alive in leaders everywhere. It's important to note that not every excellent leader is a high-flying CEO or modern day hero. Splendid examples are all around us. You'll find them in businesses, schools, churches, communities, and charities. Each of the following chapters is filled with stories about real people—people of incredible stature and others just like you and me. And at the end of each chapter you'll find "practical tactical" tips on how you can incorporate each commandment into your leadership efforts.

Inspire, Persuade, Lead will be a useful book for anyone who has a vision and a desire to engage people in a shared mission. It will help inspire people to action with a clear, vivid picture of success. It will help create better organizational efficiency and stronger teamwork. And it will help individual leaders build a personal savings bank of goodwill with the people important to their success.

Commandment #1: Know Yourself

> Above all else, know thyself.
> —Socrates

LEADERSHIP IS A JOURNEY THAT STARTS WHEN YOU MUSTER UP THE COURAGE TO BE HONEST WITH YOURSELF. It should go without saying, but *telling the truth* is the most fundamental element of leadership communication. Of course, individual politicians, journalists, lawyers, scholars, and theologians all have different perspectives on the truth. Keeping all the facts in place is certainly important. But the core of Commandment #1 isn't about the kind of truth that can be investigated and defended. It's about being true to yourself.

Every leader has experienced at least one insightful moment when he or she has discovered his or her own truth. Probably several. And as the saying goes, sometimes *the truth hurts*. But that's OK. It keeps us humble, and it reminds us that the journey requires a great deal of courage. One of my favorite sayings is this:

Courage is fear that's said its prayers.

Most of us have a pretty good handle on what we believe to be our charms and our passions. You know, the things inside your head that make you feel good about being you. And, we probably have a decent understanding of what other people like about us—what is endearing, attractive, and admired. But it's the baggage—the stuff that others really *don't like* about us—that can be tough to handle. Exceptional leaders understand their effect on the people around them, and they understand how to use the negatives as well as the positives.

There are many different psychological tools available to help people understand themselves, including the Myers-Briggs Type Indicator (MBTI)®, DiSC Personal Profile System®, California Psychological Inventory (CPI)®, and 360-degree feedback evaluations, among others.[1] In my experience, the best way to develop a sense of knowing yourself is to gather information from three different sources:

- a personality inventory you complete yourself (Myers-Briggs, DiSC);
- an assessment completed by the people around you (360-degree); and,
- your intuition.

The tough part is putting the information into action. Understanding yourself will help you organize your day differently, set priorities for personal and professional development, and even choose the most refreshing vacation. But most importantly, it can truly help you communicate better with the people important to your success.

---

[1] The Myers-Briggs Type Indicator®, MBTI®, California Psychological Inventory® and CPI® are registered trademarks of Consulting Psychologists Press, Inc. The DiSC Personal Profile System is a registered trademark of Carlson Learning Company.

The Humble Sandwich®

To help leaders translate self-understanding into better communication, I created the Humble Sandwich®. The Humble Sandwich is a simple tool that directs your thinking to a specific audience. Here's how it works. A typical sandwich has two pieces of bread with something interesting in the middle. For the Humble Sandwich, the "bread" is the understanding of things *positive*, and the stuff in the middle is the understanding of things *negative*.

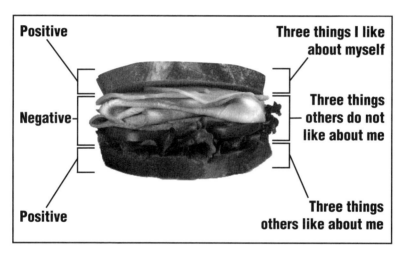

Most people order a sandwich by what's in the *middle*. Peanut butter and jelly. Ham and Swiss. Philly beef and cheese. But just like a well-built Reuben, the bread is important in a Humble Sandwich. Let's build one.

The top layer is made up of the *three things you like about yourself*. It's important that you can identify with crystal clarity the things that make you glad to be you—your qualities, your passions. Here's my top layer:

Three things I like about myself:

1. I'm good at many things.

2. I'm creative.

3. I love teaching people new things.

Throughout my career, these three things have remained constant.

The bottom layer is based on what you've learned in written evaluations and from your gut that you know *other people like about you.* Here's my bottom layer:

The three things I know others like about me:

1. I spread enthusiasm.

2. I'm a good "coach."

3. I'm creative.

Finally, it's important to think about the people important to your success and identify the things that they *don't like* about you. This step is very important. In times of tension or misunderstanding, people tend to focus on the negative. If you don't recognize and acknowledge the negative factors influencing your leadership, communication will suffer. Here's the *"messy stuff in the middle"* for me:

The three things I know others don't like about me:

1. I have a high degree of confidence, which can be perceived as arrogant or cocky.

2. Sometimes I move too fast, not being careful enough to include others.

3. I tend to make more promises than I can follow through on.

When I'm communicating with people who don't know me very well, understanding this information helps. But the most important part of using the messy stuff in the middle is to understand that it can change with different audiences.

As you can see for yourself, I need to use my Humble Sandwich to keep my ego in check! There are people who are attracted by the energy of that natural style. But more often than not, those instincts need to be kept in check by thinking ahead, slowing down, and looking for a broader perspective. The Humble Sandwich changed my life, and it can change your life too.

Here's a full picture of my Humble Sandwich. Use the blank spaces that follow to build your own.

Three things I like about myself:

1. I'm good at many things.

2. I'm creative.

3. I love teaching people new things.

The three things I know others don't like about me:

1. I have a high degree of confidence, which can be perceived as arrogant or cocky.

2. Sometimes I move too fast, not being careful enough to include others.

3. I tend to make more promises than I can follow through on.

The three things I know others like about me:

1. I spread enthusiasm.

2. I'm a good "coach."

3. I'm creative.

Now it's your turn.

Three things I like about myself:

1. _____
_____

2. _____
_____

3. _____
_____

The three things I know others don't like about me:

1. _____
_____

2. _____
_____

3. _____
_____

The three things I know others like about me:

1. _____
_____

2. _____
_____

3. _____
_____

Growing Into Your Style

It's hard to fully understand your full impact on people until you break out of your routine and try something different. To truly understand yourself, you have to get outside the ordinary and try new things. People who work and live in the same environments for a long time tend to repeat their behaviors and "pigeon-hole" themselves. I see people with terrific leadership potential limit themselves with artificial constraints because they haven't stretched themselves beyond the boundaries of their everyday environment. Often those boundaries are set within their own mind—not in others.

You can break out of your routine and discover yourself in any number of ways. Follow your passions and volunteer. Coach a team, mentor a young person, join a nonprofit board of directors, or take a college class. You'll advance your ability to communicate as you explore the depths of who you are.

You Gotta' Have Heart

"One day I found myself running a $350-million-dollar not-for-profit corporation, an experience I could have never gotten through my job. And it all started from the energy of knowing I made a difference," said David Ness, a quiet, soft-spoken Scandinavian who can be admired for many things. He is a top executive at Medtronic, one of America's golden success stories. Over a 28-year career, he's helped propel Medtronic to the top of the "best places to work in America" list several times. He's seen the company grow from around 500 employees in Fridley, Minnesota, to more than 28,000 worldwide.

In the course of those 28 years, he's managed to stay fulfilled and challenged inside the company. But it didn't all come from one source. David has accepted leadership challenges in his community, in his church, and most significantly with the American Heart Association, where he eventually held the position of national chairman.

"Well, as a Scandinavian Lutheran, what I'm going to suggest is probably the opposite of what you would expect to hear!" he grinned. "I think the key to knowing yourself is to find your passion. Out of the last 13 years, more so than the previous 15 years, I've learned that you lead better when you are passionate. Passion is without a doubt the most powerful thing."

So how, exactly, does David define passion?

Passion is energy. The parallels between the American Heart Association and Medtronic create that energy for me. When personal and professional values connect, you simply can't hold back the passion. You can't hold back the energy—it naturally brings your best skills to the forefront. And that's really important, because often I've seen people guarding themselves, feeling like they have to protect themselves. But if you are passionate, you can't hold back your natural energy, your passion.

Looking back, for the first 15 years, I worked hard and practiced my trade. I'm an analytical person, very comfortable with numbers, very comfortable with thought processes—I can do that in my head. But I wasn't really leading people. I think, as you get older, you move from the head to the heart and you really find your ability to lead.

Again, my connection the American Heart Association tells the story for me.

When I first got involved 18 years ago, I intended to stay for three meetings. They needed my help in changing their statewide benefits program. We saved the employees over 50 percent, and increased their benefits threefold. But more importantly, it hit me that I'd really made a difference. They allowed me to contribute, and they made me feel good about it. So the feeling, at the end of the day, was that I'd done something that I wouldn't have otherwise done and I did it better than others maybe could have done it. I became passionate about the cause, the momentum got started, and eventually I became the national chair.

Leading from the Side of the Table

"When I discovered I could be more powerful leading people from the side of the table than from the front, my life opened up," explained Terri Sullivan, a bright thinker and passionate community contributor with the Search Institute. Terri built her career in the public relations industry. As a partner in a prominent national firm, she rose to a senior position at a young age. "I vividly remember the pressure of having young, bright people under my authority," she explained. "They expected so much from me and it was frightening! I never really saw myself as a leader, although I tried to be what they needed. Then one day I came to grips with the specific expectations of the people who reported to me. I realized that's not me! It took courage, but it was exhilarating."

Along that journey, Terri received advice from mentors who helped her to know herself better. "Someone told me that people don't always need to be at the top to lead," she recalled. "Organizations need all kinds of leaders at all levels. That advice allowed me to play the good cop role. Sometimes when you are in a real position of authority, you have to play the bad cop. I just couldn't handle it. I lead better from the side of the table, in a mentor or coaching role."

That self-realization launched a career in community building with the Search Institute, a nationally prominent nonprofit whose driving force is building assets in children. They provide communities with information, research tools, communication expertise, and strategic planning help to create better places for young people to live and grow. Terri has been instrumental in launching strategic planning initiatives where community leaders, politicians, schools, families, and kids work together to build assets. "It's a far cry from the billable-by-the-hour consulting days," she laughed. "You can't just barge in and say 'this is what I think!' That's definitely not leadership in this world. Things move slowly, but you can create lasting change when you get people working and thinking together. And that's more my style."

"What Terri Sullivan and David Ness discovered about themselves is absolutely critical to their leadership," advised Sandra Davis, Ph.D. Sandra is the founder and CEO of MDA Consulting Group, a world-class leadership development firm headquartered in Minneapolis, Minnesota. She is the co-author of *Reinventing Yourself* (Consulting Psychologists Press, 1998) with Bill Handschin.

"Many people have transformed their work life through volunteer experiences. Volunteer work can be highly rewarding. It gives people a chance to hone their skills, learn new skills, and spread their wings," Sandra explained. "For some people, that leads to discovering who they are. Whether or not they are comfortable making high-level decisions. Whether or not certain career activities are fulfilling. The key is to recognize the connection between our personalities and how much we enjoy working in a certain job, assuming a certain role, working towards a meaningful end."

Sandra is a top executive coach, advising CEOs and other leaders on strategies for navigating challenging life and work situations. "Leadership is really a developmental journey. A constant learning process about who you really are, what you envision you can become, and how you affect other people."

One of the fundamental tools Sandra uses is the Myers-Briggs Type Indicator. The MBTI is a staple in leadership coaching. It helps people put personality theories into practical application. "At some point, every leader learns that communicating with people who are not like themselves is difficult," Sandra explained. "The MBTI gives leaders a lens for understanding themselves and other people—how they process information, how they look at the world, the elements of their job that are interesting and important to them, and how communication styles can make a big difference. In the most basic sense, the turn-on and turn-off triggers when it comes to word choices and communication styles. But it all starts with understanding yourself."

Commandment #1
Practical Tactical Tips

Try these practical tactical tips to help you apply *Commandment #1: Know Yourself* to your leadership:

Create your own Humble Sandwich.

Photocopy the Humble Sandwich exercise from this chapter, or visit *www.leaderbuilder.net* and download the Humble Sandwich Builder. If you have the Myers-Briggs Type Indicator, 360-Degree feedback, or other psychological information available to you, use it to help develop your Humble Sandwich. Then, share your Humble Sandwich with a trusted colleague for an honest review.

Identify your passions.

Write down the projects or assignments that brought you the most energy. Ask yourself: *How can I create more of that energy in my life?*

Ask a colleague: When am I at my best?

This is the most straightforward way to hone in on your leadership strengths. Listen carefully to the answer, and ask yourself: *How can I create more situations like that in my leadership journey?*

BONUS
Use the Leadership Communication Self-Test.

Leadership Communication Self-Test

How do you think the people important to your success will rate your leadership communication? A self-test can help you determine how you score. Take the test yourself, and then ask the people important to your success to evaluate you as well. Compare the results for a reality check and to guide your development.

Skill Set	Evaluation			
	Always 5	Mostly 4	Not Enough 2	Almost Never 1
1. Do you understand your impact on people, and adjust your approach accordingly?				
2. Do you tailor your communication techniques based on your audience?				
3. Do you address pre-existing barriers before trying to forge ahead?				
4. Do you tell meaningful stories to provide clarity and context for change?				
5. Do you use visual techniques to illustrate important concepts?				

Skill Set	Evaluation			
	Always 5	Mostly 4	Not Enough 2	Almost Never 1
6. Do you practice *no surprises* by regularly forecasting and closing the loop?				
7. Do you take the time to put important items down in writing to facilitate agreement?				
8. Do you intentionally choose language that accurately describes what you are thinking?				
9. Do you intentionally spread enthusiasm for the positive?				
10. Do you avoid getting defensive when challenged by colleagues and employees?				

Total Points: _____

Scoring

MASTER: 40 points or higher—You set an excellent example. You will improve your organization if you actively teach these skills to others.

ADVANCED: 30-39 points—You are better than most, and could be excellent if you seek out feedback from others and apply your learning.

INTERMEDIATE: 20-29 points—Your skills are underdeveloped. Be courageous, and look at every encounter as an opportunity to improve. Even the smallest changes will make a big difference.

Commandment #2: Understand Your Audience

Seeing things with a fresh perspective is one of
the greatest joys of being alive.
—Sculptor Paul T. Granlund

KEEN LISTENING AND SHARP OBSERVATIONS ARE GIFTS
THAT WILL BRING MANY RETURNS. Excellent leaders
have the Midas touch because they appreciate the
importance of empathy—truly *understanding* people.
They take the time to know the dreams, goals, and
values of people important to their success. When
speaking on this subject, there are always a few
people in the back of the room who are sending me
the signal that says: *Yeah, yeah, we've all heard this
listening stuff a hundred times before.*

The problem is that even though most people
have heard it before, they continue to be very poor
listeners. Why is listening so important? The answer
is simple: People need to feel appreciated. It's that
basic. Ask any successful traveler through France
how important it is to understand the French language and appreciate the French culture. Even a
feeble attempt to demonstrate understanding will

take you a long way. When people don't feel understood or appreciated, they get irritated, resentful, and ultimately become disengaged. And if you have disengaged people on your team, it's definitely *your* problem.

Is the Golden Rule Really Golden?

In time, talented leaders eventually discover that the Golden Rule as we all learned it—*do unto others as you would have them do unto you*—doesn't work very well in communication. Effective leadership requires communication that is receiver-focused—communication in their language, at their pace, in the style that works best for *them*—not you.

An eager, young leader learned this lesson the hard way. He was energetic, visionary and loved people. At 32 years of age, he had just achieved his first role as chief technology officer in a $50-million technology company. He flew in from Boston on Sunday night, and first thing Monday morning he called a "stand-up meeting." He introduced himself and pledged to create an open environment with a free flow of communication. He asked what people thought and no one answered. He asked for questions and no one said anything.

"It's just my first day on the job he thought . . . we'll do it again tomorrow and it will go much better." Again, Tuesday at 9 a.m., he called another stand-up meeting. The same thing happened. After two weeks of uncomfortable, unproductive stand-up meetings, a communication consultant pointed out three obvious mistakes in his approach.

First, in Boston many people start their workday at 9 a.m. This was the hearty Midwest, most of the technology team had arrived before 7:30 a.m., and were heavily into their day's work when he called them away from their desks. Second, while he was invigorated by group conversation and brainstorming, the technology team was comprised of computer and electrical engineers. Mostly introverts. Each was originally hired by a quiet, intellectually driven leader. When the consultant asked the technology team to comment on the stand-up meetings, almost everyone replied "I hate meetings, and I don't like talking in front of other people."

Third, and most important, the technology team thought sending e-mails was the best way to share information. Conversations were for social information. E-mails were specific, could be printed, and would allow for an exchange of ideas when they had time to participate on their own schedule. These people were driven by the creative process—inventing, testing, and stretching their minds. When they were in the groove, they didn't want to be interrupted. The most pointed comment was this: "I get paid to solve technical problems for customers. When I'm standing up outside my cube in the middle of the day there's a customer waiting, and one of our competitors is probably dreaming up something that will make our technology obsolete. Send me an e-mail and I'll get back to you when I've got time."

The feedback was a hard pill to swallow for the young CTO. He didn't understand his audience. Fortunately for him, the consultant helped him alter his personal style and build a leadership communication strategy that best suited his team, which helped him succeed.

The young CTO could have used two simple methods—personality profiling and the Five Languages of Appreciation to help him succeed. First, let's talk about personality profiling.

Understanding Personality Profiling

Thousands of years ago, the Egyptians realized that people were not all alike. They identified four basic personality types and labeled them with references to nature—earth, wind, water, and fire—and they associated each personality with colors. Earth was green, wind was yellow, water was blue, and fire was red. Not surprisingly, they discovered that different personality types were drawn to certain functions in their society. The best military leaders were fire/red, and the best politicians were water/blue.

In many ways, we've evolved significantly since the Egyptians, but just like then, people differ today. Can you spot the difference in personalities? Do you know the difference between a "thinker" and a "feeler"? How about the difference between a "talker" and a "doer"? The terms *thinker, feeler, talker,* and *doer* are a little more descriptive than the descriptions used by the Egyptians, and they represent a very simple methodology for personality profiling. The most important element is to recognize that people are not alike, and they don't process information the same way.

Think back: The young CTO didn't realize that he was a talker and his technology team was made up of thinkers. It's very basic, yet the majority of poor leaders try to communicate only from their own personality style. Many companies actually reinforce this type of inflexibility—they simply hire people who "fit in." For decades some of America's largest companies have been making it a standard practice to hire people with very similar personality types. They actually test them before hiring, and choose those who best fit the mold. This works great as long as things always stay the same.

Remember the famous blue-suit-and-white-shirt company? Many leaders inside the old IBM developed a couple of communication techniques that worked with most everyone. But when the times changed, and a different type of employee and customer emerged, those singular skills were exposed. Pick up *Fast Company, Red Herring,* or *Wired* magazine. Almost every issue has an article emphasizing open communication as a key to succeeding in the modern economy. To be nimble, your organization needs leaders who can adapt their style to the people who are important to their success.

Meeting the Basic Types

Jesse Ventura, Oprah Winfrey, Alan Greenspan, and Hillary Clinton are all very dynamic personalities. Let's look at what makes them different from a personality profiling perspective.

GUARDED
Task

Thinker	**Doer**
HOW	**NOW**
WE	**ME**
Feeler	**Talker**

INDIRECT
Ask

DIRECT
Tell

OPEN
Emotion

The Talker

Minnesota governor and former World Wrestling Federation celebrity Jesse Ventura is a "talker." The key word used to describe the talker is *ME*. Jesse attracts attention even when he doesn't want to attract attention. He thinks exceptionally well on his feet, although he often says things in public that he hasn't thought through completely. Jesse enjoys calling attention to his past accomplishments and forecasting what he thinks he can accomplish tomorrow. Jesse Ventura is successful and admired by many for these qualities.

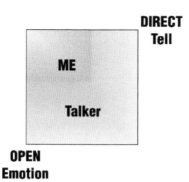

Talkers are expressive and direct in their communication. They are the most likely of all four personalities to initiate conversation, and they are more interested in people than tasks. Talkers typically have a short attention span for details and are more focused on themselves in interactions. They tend to come to conclusions by hearing themselves talk out loud. Advertising executives, sales people, and entrepreneurs are people who typically represent the talker personality. When the talker asks you, "What time is it?" they won't necessarily wait to hear your answer, but they will probably notice your watch and ask you where you bought it. And then they will tell you where they bought theirs!

Talker Communication Tips

If you are trying to persuade a talker, it's important that you:

- Intentionally let them "talk themselves out"; they tend to think out loud.

- Bring a new idea—or ask them for a new idea.

- Be attentive to their energy level—if they are "up," try to be up. If they are down, they will really appreciate you if you can re-energize them.

- Let them know their unique contribution to the situation—maybe even show them it was really *their* idea.

- Circle back and summarize what you've covered—talkers are not good at translating conversations into details. Be specific about what you need and when.

You'll hurt your chances for success if you:

- Ask for long meetings or hold long conversations.
- Send long, detailed e-mails or voicemails.
- Cut them off in the middle of a good idea or story—they need to feel like they are heard.
- Present a carefully organized, 27-page, bullet-point presentation to review—talkers will be bored to tears.
- Ask them to proofread or check an important technical document.

With talkers, remember the key concept: *It's about ME, my contributions are important and I'm making a difference.*

The Thinker

Alan Greenspan, the chairman of the Federal Reserve, is an example of a "thinker" personality. The key word used to describe people like him is *HOW*. Alan is a soft-spoken, analytical, intellectually driven person who has demonstrated a magnificent capacity to grasp a very complicated subject—the U. S. economy. When he speaks, he uses carefully chosen words. And when presented with a problem to solve, he will revert inward, taking time to review information and contemplate the consequences. He is successful, and admired by many for these qualities.

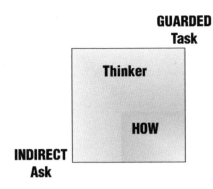

Thinkers are indirect in their communication, likely to wait to get back and respond to you. They are tight-lipped with information and are primarily interested in just the tasks at hand. The *how* best describes them because they are very detail oriented, preferring to know how you arrived at the answer before you give an answer. Librarians, accountants, and engineers are people who typically represent the "thinker" personality. Thinkers are highly analytical, and excel at research, technical writing, and complicated tasks. When a thinker asks you, "What time is it?" the thinker will expect you to tell them how the clock was built—it matters to them.

Thinker Communication Tips

If you are trying to persuade a thinker, it's important that you:

- Be organized and have a clear agenda for your interactions.
- Demonstrate clear thinking and your respect for process.
- Have proper information to back up your ideas.
- Present carefully, from a clear beginning to a well-articulated end.
- Ask them to help you "think something through."

- Limit the "chit chat"; stay away from anything too personal.

You'll hurt your chances for success if you:

- Surprise them—make sure you keep them hyper-informed.
- Skip critical details in your logic chain.
- Try to get them to "open up" about their personal lives.
- Talk too loud, too fast, or with too much emotion.

With thinkers, remember the key concept: *It's about HOW, I need to know the details.*

The Doer

Former First Lady and current New York Senator Hillary Clinton is an example of a "doer" personality. The key word used to describe people like her is *NOW*. Hillary is a driver, very direct in her approach to people, and she has shown capacity for getting many things done. She has tremendous resolve under pressure, and is able to put aside emotions to make quick, calculating decisions. She is not obsessed with details, preferring to stay focused on the big picture—making decisions by looking at "black and white" issues, not gray. She is successful and admired by many for these qualities.

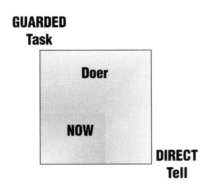

Doers are direct in their communication, likely to initiate conversation or put their hand out for a handshake ahead of you. They are usually guarded about personal information, but forthcoming with information about the task at hand. They usually ask short, direct questions, and expect answers short and to the point. Doers are not patient people, and they expect people to be efficient with their communication. They typically make good decisions by gut feelings, and accept risk easily. Security workers, military leaders, and investment bankers are people who typically represent the doer personality. When the doer asks you, "What time is it?" the doer expects one thing— you tell them the time. Anything else is unnecessary and a waste of productive time.

Doer Communication Tips

If you are trying to persuade a doer, it's important that you:

- Plan for short, tightly organized interactions.

- Respect their time—ask "how's your schedule; is this a good time to talk"?

- Get to the point—highlight the important issues, then ask what details they want.

- Show that you are in command of your subject— demonstrate that you understand the risks and rewards related to your subject.

- Stay tightly focused—doers don't like to interpret long stories or data on the fly.

You'll hurt your chances for success if you:

- Overstay your welcome—if they give you 10 minutes, don't take 15.

- Expect them to share in your personal life—they don't like to do that in the business setting.

- Ask them to participate in a spontaneous "brainstorm" for new ideas.

- Talk them through a carefully organized, 27-page, bullet-point presentation; they like to know you have it, but they won't want to see it.

With doers, remember the key concept: *It's about NOW, I don't have time for extras.*

The Feeler

Oprah Winfrey is an example of a "feeler" personality. The key word used to describe people like her is *WE*. Oprah Winfrey is the most successful television talk show host in history for a reason. She is amiable, an exceptional listener who is capable of creating private moments with people in front of millions of television viewers with empathy. She can sort through complicated human relationships and ask tough questions with sensitivity that will elicit a response. And she has revealed her own life—the good and the bad—for everyone to see. Oprah Winfrey is successful and admired by many for these qualities.

**INDIRECT
Ask**

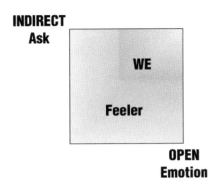

**OPEN
Emotion**

Feelers are indirect in their communication and primarily focused on people. Feelers are very aware of the people around them, ask a lot of questions, and do not like tension. They tend to make decisions by creating a consensus and making sure that everyone is OK with each other. Career counselors, customer service, social service and healthcare workers are people who typically represent the feeler personality. When the feeler asks you, "What time is it?" they will listen closely to your answer and probably respond with "I wish we had more time together."

Feeler Communication Tips

If you are trying to persuade a feeler, it's important that you:

- Make time for "chit chat"—they like to share the highs and lows.

- Bring something personal to the conversation—they really want to connect with you on an individual level.

- Demonstrate that you are not working alone—you have gathered the support of others, or intend to get the support of others after your conversation.

- Show them you are excited and engaged in your work.

- Ask for their help in creating an environment where others will welcome your ideas.

You'll hurt your chances for success if you:

- Skip the "how-are-you-doing?" part of the interaction.
- Surprise them by asking for an important decision in five minutes. It's better to tell them you need their time to talk through something—15 minutes is the minimum.
- Go "behind their back" when trying to get things done. They need to know who you are involving—consensus is very important to feelers.
- Jump to conclusions—they want to be involved in your decision-making.

With feelers, remember the key concept: *It's about how WE are getting along together.*

The point is this: If you had to enlist the support of Jesse Ventura and Alan Greenspan, you wouldn't use the same approach. If you needed the help of Oprah Winfrey and Hillary Clinton, you'd need two separate strategies. This sounds so simple, but most mediocre leaders treat everyone the same way. They try to influence everyone with the same strategy and same set of tools.

Learning from Lawyers

Trial lawyers have been putting personality profiling to work forever. They know that impassioned emotional appeals backfire as often as they work with a jury. On the flip side, logical, analytical approaches can fail as well. How do they know which strategy to choose? By learning the personality of each juror during jury selection. They watch very carefully how people are dressed. They notice how they walk, sit, and groom themselves. They notice whether shoes are shined and if fingernails are painted. They listen carefully to *how* people answer questions, as well as *what they say w*hen they answer questions. Everything is a clue into whether a person is analytical or emotional, open or guarded.

Relationship Issues or Poor Performance?

A substantial client suddenly stopped all activity with a firm and didn't explain why. The firm was busy, should the relationship be left for dead? The partner in charge was a thinker—an exceptional writer and someone who really got excited about new challenges, especially when there was a new industry to learn. He was particularly frustrated that the client didn't articulate its dissatisfaction. The second partner in the firm was a talker; he wanted to get face-to-face as soon as possible to see what went wrong.

By using personality profiling, the partners realized the two client contacts were both feelers—two people who were driven mostly by relationships. The client felt the partners had overstepped the bounds on a particular assignment, while the partners felt they had "gone the extra mile." Several weeks had gone by and the client hadn't hired anyone else to do the work; they simply were afraid to talk about their dissatisfaction.

Finally, when schedules would allow, the partners and client got together. Within minutes, the client contacts expressed genuine regret for not talking sooner. They talked about feeling uncomfortable without open, honest communication. The conflict was a relationship issue, not a performance issue. With that out in the open, the partners spent 45 minutes collecting assignments to bring home. The partners—a talker and a thinker—were the perfect team. The combination of the two personalities was effective in resolving a difficult and important relationship issue.

Personality profiling really works. Anthony Alessandra and Michael J. O'Connor wrote a terrific book, *The Platinum Rule: Discover the Four Basic Business Personalities—and How They Can Lead You to Success* (Warner Books, 1998). It's one of the best, most thorough examinations of how to apply what the Egyptians discovered thousands of years ago about earth, wind, water, and fire personalities.

Understanding the Five Languages of Appreciation

Another simple tool to help you understand your audience comes from a book called *The Five Love Languages* (Northfield Publications, 1992) by Dr. Gary Chapman. Dr. Chapman has written and lectured extensively about the Five Languages of Love that people use to give and receive love for one another. I've tweaked the Five Languages of Love to the Five Languages of Appreciation for application with business audiences. I use the Five Languages to help people understand how to give and receive *appreciation* in the work setting. Why? Because if one of the basic principles of leadership is the ability to build confidence and make people feel good about themselves, it's critical to show appreciation in a language that resonates with the individuals important to your success.

The Five Languages are:

- Words of encouragement.
- Acts of service.
- Gift giving.
- Quality time.
- Physical touch and closeness.

Typically, one of these five jumps off the page, evoking a "Yep, that's me!" response. Which one did that for you? It's important to know that about yourself, because you probably use that technique the most with others. And, you probably didn't even realize that at least one of these Five Languages wasn't very appealing to you.

Until I discovered the Five Languages, I never understood why I would get embarrassed when I received gifts. Gifts from colleagues, co-workers—even family and friends. Honestly, sometimes it actually hurt inside when I realized someone had spent so much money, or given so much of himself to give me a gift. And I certainly didn't understand that my embarrassment could appear to be ungracious to the giver. My preferences for giving and receiving appreciation are *words of encouragement* and *quality time*. Neither of those is fulfilled through gift giving. By simply learning this about myself, I've learned to accept gifts better, and share my appreciation for the people important to my success in different ways.

Speaking Their Language

Tim Schmidt is a terrific young leader who applies the Five Languages every day in his work as managing partner for Thrivent Financial for Lutherans. He learned the Five Languages concept through his work in the church, but he's integrated it into his daily leadership toolbox. He takes the time to help every new person in his firm identify what language speaks best to them. "My job as a leader is easier and more satisfying now that I understand the language that's most comfortable for every person in our firm," he explained. With more than 50 people to manage, that's a real challenge.

To get people engaged in the concept, he starts the discussion with a real-life example, citing the differences between himself and his wife, Jeanette. "My wife and I use very different languages to show appreciation for each other. We're basically polar opposites. The language that speaks best to me is near the bottom of her list. And the one that speaks best to her is dead last on my list! We really need to work hard, and go out of our way to make sure we connect," he said. Tim engages his staff in discussions about situations where the Five Languages play a part in their lives. Here are some of the real life stories that have resulted from his discussions.

Is It Simply Ambition?

A faithful young research assistant has been putting in a lot of extra time lately, arriving before 8 a.m. and staying well past 5 p.m. There was always plenty of work to fill the time. The leader spent most of her time with clients and colleagues away from the office. She was an excellent communicator, diligent in keeping her staff informed by telephone, voicemail, and e-mail.

One day she arrived at the office well past 6 p.m. and found the assistant hard at work. Her first response was, "Hey, what are you still doing here? You're working way too hard. Why don't you stop and go home to that lovely family of yours." The assistant replied, "I was just hoping we could talk about that new project." The leader said: "Oh, it's not that important—it can wait until tomorrow. I'll call you from the airport and we can go over all the details in the morning."

The leader felt good about sending the assistant home. The assistant left dejected and dissatisfied, because he was craving some *quality time* with the leader. The disconnect? The leader was excellent at using *words of encouragement* to show appreciation—she inspired most people. The bright young assistant needed *quality time* to feel appreciated. He arrived early and stayed late, specifically seeking 15 minutes of quality time to "connect" with the leader.

Are Diamonds Really Forever?

A very successful businessman enjoys buying expensive jewelry for his wife on special occasions. But over time, he realized that she very seldom wore the gifts, and her waning enthusiasm for those special little boxes concerned him. He's puzzled as to why she tears open the card with excitement and often waits for minutes before unwrapping his gift. Finally, he mustered up the courage to ask why. His wife admitted that the jewelry never really mattered to her. She has always preferred the cards, and *especially* the inscriptions he wrote specifically to her—the "how" and "why" he loved her. In fact, she's kept every single card he ever gave her. Her language is *words of encouragement;* his is *gift giving.* During 20 years of marriage, he's spent thousands on jewelry when he could have simply spent a few dollars on cards instead.

When Is Service to Others Too Selfish?

The firm had just finished the best year ever. People were working hard and really enjoying the work. Toward the end of the day, the CEO sent a "congratulations" e-mail, announcing the most profitable year ever, with bonuses twice as large as last year. People came pouring out of their offices, shaking hands, with "high-fives" and hugs all around. A spontaneous party ensued with champagne, music, and even some dancing. After more than an hour, the CEO's absence was impossible to ignore. One of the partners found the CEO hunkered down, dutifully preparing the report to the shareholders. Everything needed to be perfect—every dot and comma just right. "Let the party go on without me," he said. "My job is to make sure that the report gets done right so we can start our new year tomorrow on a good note. You go and celebrate." The partner left, thinking the leader was a Scrooge. So did everyone else.

This leader thought the best way to show appreciation to others in the firm was to work the "hardest." Putting in the longest hours, doing the most difficult tasks, and taking the least of the credit—communicating through *acts of service.* The people in the firm thought the leader was cold and out of touch. Especially in the time of celebration, most people in the firm craved a handshake, a pat on the back, and words of congratulations.

In each of these real-world stories, the person thought they were sending a specific message—but that message wasn't received in the way they expected or assumed it would be received. Reading about these techniques is easy; applying the learning is tricky.

It's All in the Cards

Tim Schmidt has a technique that helps put the Five Languages to work in his leadership. For every person in his firm, he created a wallet-sized laminated card that he uses for daily reference. Each card is complete with a photograph, full contact information, names of family members, birth date, wedding anniversary, the date they started with the firm, and the appreciation language that speaks best to them. "The cards help me stay focused on the things that really count with people," he explained. "Not everyone needs to get together face-to-face to be energized. I have people who get just as much energy from a quick, well-timed message left on the answering machine as they do from a personal visit. And others like to receive special mementos or news clippings in the mail (gift-giving). As leaders, we have so many different ways to spend our time. I try my hardest to make sure people are connected and feel appreciated in ways that work best for them."

Commandment #2
Practical Tactical Tips

Try these practical tactical tips to help you apply *Commandment #2: Understand Your Audience* to your leadership:

> **Determine the dominant personality type of the people important to your success.**
>
> Then stop and think: *Am I the same personality?* Make a list of the thinkers, feelers, doers, and talkers around you, and develop your own strategy for how to communicate with them in the style most appropriate to them. Introduce the concept at a company-wide meeting, and make a game of it. Draw caricatures of the different types on a flip chart, and develop communication scenarios in your business that will help people understand how to put personality profiling to work.
>
> **Identify the languages of appreciation for the people around you.**
>
> Write the Five Languages on a sheet of paper and ask each person—What speaks best to you? Or use the short test in Dr. Chapman's book. Keep track of how each person responds. Then, look for a moment to show your appreciation—a birthday, a project well done, a performance review—and then show your appreciation according to their preference, not yours.

Hire a consultant to administer the Myers-Briggs Type Indicator inside your organization.

Develop a chart that helps people in your organization understand the individual personalities. Use the information to resolve conflicts and build better teamwork. (This will also help support Commandment #1.)

Commandment #3:
Disarm Upfront

Our critics are our friends, because they do show us our faults.

—-Thomas Jefferson

AT THE HEIGHT OF THE MONICA LEWINSKI SCANDAL, PRESIDENT CLINTON ECHOED THESE FAMOUS WORDS, first spoken by Thomas Jefferson 200 years earlier. *"Our critics are our friends, because they do show us our faults."* But it fell on deaf ears. He never did admit his faults, he just admitted that he had misled—after the fact. A skillful politician, Bill Clinton was able to maintain favorable public opinion during one of the most serious—and definitely the most publicized—scandals in the history of the White House. But the history books won't forget his legacy of philandering and deceit. Things could have been different for him, if he understood the power of *Commandment #3: Disarm Upfront.*

Let's go back to the Humble Sandwich. Remember the "messy stuff" in the middle? How might Clinton have used that to help him in difficult times? When news of "Monicagate" was first brewing, Clinton could have pulled his staff together and said something like this:

I have made many mistakes in my life, some affecting me and some affecting lots of other people. And it's just like me to let my own ego get in the way, putting my own needs above everyone else, and now I'm afraid I've done something I'm not very proud of . . . You've probably heard rumors about my involvement with Monica Lewinski, and yes, some of them are true. It's not something I'm proud of, and I'm sorry for the pain it's going to cause my family and the trouble it will cause all of you here today.

Ouch! A speech like that to his closest advisors, family, and friends would have really taken courage. But not as much courage as it took to look them in the eye *after* the courts and the court of public opinion had crucified him. Who knows, his political fate might not have changed one bit. However, more of his integrity would have stayed intact. Unfortunately for him, comedians for decades will consider jokes about Bill Clinton's libido too easy to pass up. And, it's quite evident that permanent damage was done to some of his most important relationships.

But how can we put this lesson to work for you? *Disarm upfront* is not about covering up lies. It's a strategy to help you manage the things about you and your style that get you into trouble—the messy stuff in the middle. And, we can all use help with that. A psychologist I know tells this story to help his clients deal with their impact on people:

Once a Man was so afraid of himself, and his effect on others that he walked around day and night with a bag on his head. He was so preoccu-pied by this fear that he didn't want anyone to really know who he was. Eventually the Man couldn't live with the stress of looking at the world from behind the bag. So, he asked his best (and only) friend to help him remove the bag. The friend replied, "Sure, but you'll be surprised at what you discover." The friend carefully lifted the bag and handed it to the Man. The Man took one look at the bag, and blushed in embarrassment. Of course, the bag was clear, fully revealing the Man all along.

Whether or not you actually had the courage (or saw the need) to build your Humble Sandwich in Commandment #1, you still can't erase the fact that people see you for how you really are. The people around you are smart—you've chosen to be around most of them! They see the good and the bad, but mostly the good. If they didn't, they wouldn't be working with you. So turn back to your Humble Sandwich, deal with the "messy stuff" in the middle, and let's put that informa-tion to work.

Let's use the messy stuff from my Humble Sandwich as an example:

The three things I know others don't like about me:

1. I have a high degree of confidence, which can be perceived as arrogant or cocky.

2. Sometimes I move too fast, not being careful enough to include others.

3. I tend to make more promises than I can follow through on.

There are several ways to use this information. First, I ask myself: *"Am I moving too fast? Is it possible that I don't look prepared, or that I could come on too strong?"* With certain people—especially thinkers and feelers—I have to really keep my energy and enthusiasm in check. And it doesn't hurt for me to acknowledge out loud: *"I know I might be a little intense right now, it's been a really good day and that always pumps me up. I'll try to calm down so we can talk. No more coffee for me . . ."*

Second, if I know that I haven't yet acted upon one of the promises I've made, I need to get that out on the table. Often, that dialogue sounds like this.

I realize the last time we talked, we agreed to move that project forward. My role was to call Mr. Right and get his approval. I haven't done it yet, although I still intend to do it. If that's holding up our ability to move forward, I'll go do it right now and we can catch up later.

I'm not trying to shed my responsibilities, or make excuses—that generally doesn't work. But by being honest upfront, I can clear the air of the tension that is bound to be present. More often than not, the person important to my success will respond, "That's OK, there's something that I haven't done either, but we can still accomplish plenty in this meeting."

Third, when tensions are high, my opinionated, aggressive style can be very cutting. Because my brain works most quickly when I'm on my feet, and I'm not always careful in choosing my words, I sometimes suffer from foot-in-mouth disease. It's exaggerated by the fact that I almost always deliver my opinion with passion. Throughout the years, I've heard from peers and through 360-degree evaluations that this can be perceived as arrogant and abrasive. Before I discovered the power of *disarm upfront,* I thought "arrogant and abrasive" were fightin' words!

For people like me, it's a good idea to let others know upfront that you have the potential to come on a little strong. Most people have an abrasive edge. You will buy yourself a little "wiggle room," and build up some credit in your savings bank of goodwill if you use your Humble Sandwich appropriately.

Disarm with Humor

Disarm upfront also can turn into lighthearted humor. Self-deprecating humor—when you take a shot at yourself—is the most endearing form of wit. It can help you be entertaining and fun to be around. Believe me, at 5' 6'' tall, many jokes have been made about my short stature. When I speak, lead strategic planning sessions, or skill-building boot camps, there's always someone in the room who is thinking: "Man, that guy's short." I know it's true because I've heard people describe me as "that short guy with the bow tie." But that information is useful and can be used as disarming, self-deprecating humor. I can joke:

- "I'm short in every way, except in confidence."
- "I'm the founding member of the short-white-smart-aleck-with-hair club for men."

- "I better stop and let my tongue catch up with what I just said."

You can use self-deprecating humor for disarming and entertaining, if you apply it sparingly and sincerely. Jesse Ventura has often said: *"Here comes the big mouth again,"* about himself. The honest humor is part of what makes him endearing to many people. Jay Leno said one evening on the *Tonight Show: "Sorry if I seem a little unprepared tonight . . . I got to the studio really late; it was a car accident—I collided with my chin!"*

And my personal favorite. A Rotary colleague, when delivering a speech about her meandering personal and career life, cracked a clever, disarming joke. Before explaining a very circuitous route to a successful career as a stockbroker, she disarmed by saying: *"Most people have skeletons in their closet. Mine is full of entire* bodies!"

It's Just Numbers

"There are times when this stuff looks like Greek to me too!" That's a phrase you typically won't hear from a financial professional about balance sheets. But Pam Shaw Hargrove is different. She is an enterprising leader who has an exceptional mind for finance. She has the remarkable ability to quickly understand and interpret a budget, balance sheet, or financial statement. One thing she's learned over the years is that most people can't read a balance sheet. For these people, balance sheets might as well be categorized as another language like hieroglyphics, Arabic, or Greek. And people who can read the language of a balance sheet tend to be poor communicators.

Through the years, Pam Hargrove's leadership has extended from big business into many prominent non-profit boards. Most boards consider fiscal responsibility to be their number one priority, yet most board members can't read a balance sheet. The burden of responsibility, combined with the confusion brought on by "numbers," creates tension on almost every board.

Pam is very efficient at disarming upfront. She goes out of her way to make people feel confident and respected, even though they can't follow along as quickly as she'd like. She begins by building a context for the budget—providing perspective on what happened last year at this time, and what trends are affecting the budget. With nearly every new subject, she disarms the potential confusion. She uses phrases like,

Remember, the government requires us to report that income in this quarter, even though we won't really see the money until next year. I know it doesn't make any sense, but that's the way we're required to keep track. It's confusing to me, too. There are times when I wish we could just count real money, like real money, but I'm OK with this.

By admitting that she is at times confused, and the subject can be *confusing* even for her is effectively disarming.

Part of her success is her willingness to make light-hearted jokes about her Myers-Briggs type, and how that effects her leadership. Recently she said: "I'm perfect for the financial job. My personality is an ISTJ [introverted, sensing, thinking, and judging] Myers-Briggs type.[2] For those of you who don't know what that is, the Myers-Briggs people nicknamed me 'The Inspector.' I have a hard time leaving the little things alone. There is a prayer for me, and it goes like this:

> *Lord, help me relax about insignificant details, beginning tomorrow at 11:42.23 a.m. Eastern Standard Time.*"

She added, "That's just me, isn't it?"

In every situation, Pam has become a powerful, respected leader. By skipping most of the insignificant details in the budget, and painting a broad, simple picture, Pam knows how to build up her savings bank of goodwill. So, when she makes a point to stop, slow down, and call attention to one specific detail, everyone pays attention. That's an excellent use of *disarm upfront* in leadership communication.

Identifying Triggers

A former colleague of mine was continually amazed and baffled by her performance review comments and 360-degree feedback. While most people offered high praise such as "excellent project manager" and "terrific communication skills," they almost always balanced this with noticeably poor scores on "listening to others" and "works well in teams." Probing further, people believed

---

[2]The basic indicators, which can be combined into 48 different combinations to describe different personality types, are Introversion (I), Extroversion (E), Sensing (S), Intuition (N) Thinking (T), Feeling (F), Perceiving (P), and Judging (J) personalities.

the colleague was headstrong, too quick to make judgments, and came to meetings with decisions already made. The trigger points were most often fast-moving projects where people needed to really work closely together.

After the colleague learned to disarm upfront, performance reviews—and her leadership efforts—improved over time. By learning to use phrases such as, *"You guys know that I tend to think out loud, and I need to write things down to really understand myself. So, even though I might look like my mind is already made up . . . it's really not. I really want to hear what you have to say."* That even meant learning not to think out loud until others had the chance to weigh in. Being quick to get things on paper could be perceived as controlling. The colleague learned to say, *"I just needed to see something in writing—I have very little ownership, so feel free to make this your own."* Subtle, consistent, disarming statements helped to keep the colleague's pointed style in check and improved her ability to influence others.

Effectively Using the Messy Stuff

A very successful finance person I know regularly created havoc in her organization until she discovered *disarm upfront.* She brought in a lot of money for the firm, but when she was stressed she was known for saying: *"The market is where we make money, not in the office. I don't have time for this stuff."* She may have been right, but the effect this behavior had on people who worked all day in the office was substantial. Her trigger points were volatile days in the market. With keen insight into what others *didn't like* about her, she was able to disarm upfront by starting her office encounters with statements like: *"It hasn't been a very good day today . . . the markets are going crazy, and we haven't sold anything major in awhile, so I'm feeling a little crabby. I know this is important stuff, but my mind's not really sane right now. What, specifically, can I do that will be helpful?"* In most cases, the office staff preferred she be out with clients. By taking the time to let people know what was really on her mind, she made herself human. The people in the office felt like they were appreciated and her leadership soared.

Calming Fears about "The Shrink"

Sandra Davis, whom you met in Commandment #1, coaches high-profile leaders—people who are interviewing for big jobs, or people who want to learn more about themselves for growth in their careers. "For most people, visiting any kind of psychologist can be intimidating," Sandra explained. "We go out of our way to disarm their fears and make sure people don't think we are going to 'fix' them." Of course, some people are very cynical, and need more disarming than others. If they are afraid of "visiting the psychologist," then Sandra knows they won't be receptive to learning. "We tell people: 'You won't find a couch anywhere in here,'" she said.

Commandment #3
Practical Tactical Tips

Try these practical tactical tips to help you apply *Commandment #3: Disarm Upfront,* to your leadership:

Complete your Humble Sandwich.

(Did you skip that assignment in Commandment #1?) Keep it nearby so you can put the "messy stuff in the middle" to work.

Practice disarming with these phrases:

I realize when times get tense, I tend to . . .

I've learned that in times like this, I tend to drive people crazy when I . . .

You know that sometimes I can be . . .

Review a list of the people important to your success, acknowledge the tensions and frustrations that are present, and begin by clearing the air. Allow them time to disarm too.

Counsel a colleague on how to disarm upfront.

Helping someone else apply this technique will help you understand how to apply the concept yourself.

BONUS

Review your Leadership Communication Self Test for clues as to what things should be included in your Humble Sandwich.

Commandment #4:
Tell Stories

The stories that you tell about your past shape
your future.
> —Eric Ransdell, contributing editor of
> *Fast Company*

"STORYTELLING HAS BEEN AROUND FOREVER," said
John Beardsley, chairman of Padilla Speer Beardsley
Public Relations in Minneapolis. "It's our most natural form of communication. The etchings carved on
the walls of ancient ruins were deliberate attempts to
carry stories forward. People have been sitting
around the campfire telling stories since mankind
learned how to use fire. Every person, every company,
every community has a story . . . those stories can be
told from many different perspectives. But they must
be told."

More than just entertainment and folklore, stories
play a very important role in teaching and learning.
Our stories define us and stay with us. Cognitive psychologists determined long ago that people seldom
remember anything more than the first and last item
on a typical list. Stories present a picture that is more
easily remembered—a complex chain of events, a
cause-and-effect relationship, and a point that is

easily recalled. It's amazing how a good joke can be repeated by many different people and still remain intact. The "whole" of the story is significantly more memorable than the sum of its parts because we can see ourselves involved in the story—as if we've actually been there.

Beardsley has spent more than three decades counseling leaders on the art of storytelling. "As CEOs, we need to provide perspective, to connect our past with our present, and to provide a framework by which to view our future. Storytelling is the best way to provide that perspective." Stories are powerful one-on-one, with groups of employees, with customers—in the spoken and written word. Successful enterprises intentionally articulate and pass along stories.

In the May-June 1998 issue of the *Harvard Business Review*, Gordon Shaw, Robert Brown, and Philip Bromiley co-authored an article, "Strategic Stories: How 3M is Rewriting Business Planning." The basic premise rides on the belief that bullet-point plans, while concise, present only an illusion of clarity. Stories present a more compelling leadership model, filled with vivid descriptions of the market conditions, change initiatives, and acceptable resolutions. The article begins:

> *At 3M we tell stories. Everyone knows that, in our earliest days, a share of 3M stock was worth a shot of whiskey in a local St. Paul bar. We tell stories about how we failed with our first abrasive products and stories about how we invented masking tape and Wetordry sandpaper. More recently, we've been telling the story about one of*

our scientists who, while singing in a choir, wished he had bookmarks that wouldn't fall out of the hymnal—and later created Post-it Notes.

The objective for moving to a strategic story-telling planning model is simple. They write: "The ultimate success of our plans depends on how effectively we inspire the people who make those plans happen. A well-written narrative strategy that shows a difficult situation and an innovative solution . . . is certainly more engaging than a bullet-pointed mandate to increase market share by 5 percent."

Howard Gardner, author of *Leading Minds* (Basic Books, 1996), agrees. He points out that stories open the mind to a deeper state of attentiveness. He writes: "In speaking of stories, rather than messages or themes, leaders present a dynamic perspective to their followers—not just a headline or snapshot, but a drama that unfolds over time, in which they—the leaders and followers—are the principal characters or heroes."

Getting Your Story Straight

So what makes a good story? Matt Kucharski, leader of the technology practice area at Padilla Speer Beardsley Public Relations, coaches his clients to think like Hollywood movie producers, telling their stories with the time-honored formula: Stage Setting, Conflict, Resolution, and Outcome. In a 2000 *PR Tactics* article, he writes:

Companies are in a competition for attention that's not altogether different from the battle at the summer box office. The problem is, most companies have a terrible time telling their stories, and as a result, throw a lot of money at a program with a really weak story line. The best way to tell if a company has its story straight is to ask someone in management if they can recite the 30-second "elevator story." This is the one you tell to a prospect on the ride up the elevator—also known as the "back-fence" story. If you ask the company CEO, CFO and vice president of marketing to recite the story and each one does it differently, then it's time to take them all to a good movie.

The components are basic:

- Stage Setting is where we learn about the characters, the setting, and background on how everyone got to where they are.

- Conflict refers to the important issues that have arisen and are causing problems for the characters. Most stories have conflict on several levels, between multiple characters.

- Resolution is when events happen that are designed to deal with the conflict. They can be as obvious as the final fight scene in *Gladiator* or as subtle as Kevin Spacey's life realizations at the end of *American Beauty.*

- Outcome is where we learn how life is different as a result of what's happened. Sometimes the outcome is stated, and other times it's implied or left for the viewers to draw their own conclusions

This formula works for all modern-day forums for storytelling: news releases, letters to shareholders in annual reports, advertising and marketing materials, sermons, speeches, and company meetings. To help leaders build their elevator story, Kucharski asks:

- What's the landscape today (stage setting)?
- What are the problems associated with the current methods (conflict)?
- How does your company address these (resolution)?
- What is the ultimate benefit (outcome)?

He cautions, "Most stories that are too commercial are the result of putting the resolution before the conflict." Remember, think about the story from your audience's perspective.

Stories can be used to engage employees, foster a culture, attract investors, inspire a team, ease the pain of a difficult situation, share a burden, connect a group, or persuade a customer. They can be stories managers tell again and again to hundreds, or personal stories you share one-on-one with the people important to your success. Here are a few examples of how stories have been an important part of leadership communication.

Bold Dreams

Paul Harmel is the CEO of Lifetouch, the world's largest professional photography company. Lifetouch is an American dream company, a large corporate entity driven by local involvement in the schools, churches, and retail stores. With nearly $1 billion in sales, it is one of the world's largest employee-owned companies. When speaking to more than 2,400 employee-owners and their spouses at the company's 60th anniversary celebration, Harmel stepped back in time to tell a story that shaped the moment:

> *Today, we stand 60 years proud and strong. And it's important that we all know something—our founders intended it to be this way. Eldon Rothgeb and Bruce Reinecker started this company with $500, a big dream, and a trunkload of photography equipment. They drove door to door, from school to school on dirt roads. Times were very different then, nobody knew about, or appreciated, school portraits. The equipment was big, heavy, and unreliable. But they had big dreams and they were bold in their pursuit. They called themselves "National" School Studios when they barely covered one Minnesota county. I believe today they are pleased, knowing that we are still true to their mission . . . to photograph every school child, so families can cherish those childhood memories of school for generations.*

Lifetouch has consistently grown at a double-digit pace for years, continually adding people to the company who don't know that story. Paul and other senior management tell the story every chance they get. It provides the perspective that frames the importance of their business, and it is one of the pillars of the Lifetouch culture.

It's More than Just a Job

The growth at Medtronic has been even more impressive, and storytelling has literally been a corporate strategy to support its growth. Today, with more than 28,000 employees working in 120 countries across the globe, the company that invented the pacemaker has become one of the most respected companies in the world.

"We're working extremely hard to keep the small company feel of Medtronic, providing that personal touch to our employees," explained CEO Bill George. "Many companies half our size have lost their sense of community. They have people who come to work every day to a job, taking home a paycheck. When a new job comes along with a bigger paycheck, there's nothing that encourages them to stay. We believe every employee deserves to fully understand our history, our purpose, and why our work really is the difference between life and death."

Since the earliest days of Medtronic, co-founder Earl Bakken has been meeting with every new employee hired around the world in a program called the Medallion Ceremony. Now with 28,000 employees, Bill shares the job with him. At the ceremonies, held throughout the year in different Medtronic locations, Earl and Bill share the story of how Medtronic was founded, and the company's mission and values. "It started with conversations between one, two, ten, or twelve people," Bill recalled. "Then eventually our growth meant that Earl Bakken traveled abroad, communicating the Medtronic mission to employees in different countries. Today we hold the Medallion Ceremony in Japan, India, China, and beyond. It's important that people understand that the company was founded by a man who liked to 'tinker' with what looked more like hardware than the medical devices we know today. At one point, they had 38 people working in a garage in north Minneapolis, with no heat in the winter or cooling in the summer."

Storytelling as a corporate strategy doesn't stop there for Medtronic. At the annual holiday meeting, which is the company's most important event of the year, six patients and their physicians are invited to share their stories and tell how Medtronic has given them back their physical, mental, and spiritual well being.

Building International Understanding

"The most fascinating week of my entire life came about completely by surprise," Dayton Soby explained. "One day I was a simple attorney, and the next day I was standing on the Mount of Olives, overlooking Jerusalem's Old City," he continued. "The Mount of Olives is one of the most coveted pieces of land in all of history. There is no more historic setting, a site of many famous battles and the footsteps of Christ."

As a Minneapolis attorney, Soby is deeply dedicated to community service through the Lutheran Church. His résumé includes service on his church council, the board of directors of Fairview Hospital and Health Systems, and the board of Lutheran Social Service. Dayton is a man of few words, but when he speaks, people listen. It's the perspective he shares through stories about the many challenges and battles faced in his years of service that give credibility and impact to his voice.

The fortress at the top of the Mount of Olives is Augusta Victoria Hospital, operated since the 1940s by the Lutheran World Federation (LWF), and primarily serving the needs of the Palestinian people. It was built originally as a hostel in the early 1900s by Germany's Kaiser Wilhelm II, but converted into a hospital after World War II. Dayton received a call from the head of LWF because the hospital was in a deep crisis. Funding was drying up, the hospital was losing money rapidly, and its future was in doubt.

"With the reduction in United Nations funding, Lutheran World Relief and the Evangelical Lutheran Church in America could not continue to sustain the ailing facility," Dayton explained. "I was asked to review the situation with a German doctor and make recommendations about the future of Augusta Victoria. Even though on paper I looked qualified, I felt totally unprepared."

What they found was a glaring lack of governance. No one was accepting the responsibility of running the hospital. "Because Augusta Victoria had been funded by an outside force, the free market factors that normally drive quality and efficiency had totally been ignored. The entire place was out of balance," he recalled. "I spent a lot of time telling stories about how hospitals in the West were governed. I told long, detailed stories about how decisions were made, how services were administered, how billing for services worked, and how the standards for cleanliness and care were maintained. We shared a broken version of the English language, but the stories made our conversations come to life. By the end of the week, the ad hoc administrator would say: 'Here comes another one of Dayton's stories.' I took that as a compliment."

Dayton's ability to use stories to bridge a communication gap, as well as share from his personal experiences, helped paint a picture for hospital administrators on how things might be different for patients and staff at Augusta Victoria. Without a detailed manual for "how to turn around a troubled hospital," the Palestinian leaders were able to translate Dayton's stories into real-world activities that stabilized a very difficult situation. I've heard Dayton tell the story about his experience at Augusta Victoria at different times to illustrate different points—and each time it's extremely powerful.

Telling the Stories Around You

Steve McKinley is the leader of House of Prayer Lutheran Church in a suburb of Minneapolis. He's a charming, successful pastor, gifted in many ways. But he's particularly fond of his job as "editor/writer" of the church newsletter. Most churches delegate the newsletter to an administrator, who fills it with dates, times, and notices. But McKinley has found a great return on his investment by telling the stories of the individuals in the congregation who are carrying out the Word. "A church—or any organization for that matter—is nothing but a collection of people who make marvelous contributions," he explained. "It's the people who carry out their work day by day, year by year who deserve to be celebrated." The newsletter column is called *Minister of the Month*. Here's an excerpt:

Dolores Knudsen has been nominated as our February Minister of the Month for good reason. She is one of our most faithful, dedicated volunteers. She has been involved in many "behind the scenes" ministries here at House of Prayer for many years, and behind the scenes is where she wants to be. Dolores has always had a soft spot for kids in need. She remembers one year baking over 100 cupcakes for a picnic at Minnehaha Falls for the kids at House of Prayer. The kids who knew her from the church, her neighborhood, and through her daughter's school, called her house Knudsen's Kitchen *or sometimes* Knudsen's Corner, *since they could always come over to her house and get fed and listened to and cared for. When they needed a place to stay over night, they could always go there. Many of these kids, who are now adults, stay in touch with Dolores through letters of appreciation and phone calls. She thinks of herself as the "champion of the underdog."*

Pastor McKinley wouldn't give up the Minister of the Month concept for anything. "We've really brought our faith community together by sharing the stories about who we are, what we do, and how we are all making a difference," he beamed. "And you can't argue with the burst of new energy we have around the coffee pot on the Sunday morning each month after the Minister of the Month column appears."

Commandment #4
Practical Tactical Tips

Try these practical tactical tips to help you apply *Commandment # 4: Tell Stories,* to your leadership:

Memorize the storytelling formula.

By using the formula you can build tight, effective stories. Then start by telling *your* stories. You should have at least a half dozen stories from your career or the history of your organization that you can use to invigorate your communication.

Include at least one story in every speech or significant meeting to help you grab attention and set the stage for a productive session.

Read magazines to help you identify and create stories to use in your communication. *Reader's Digest, Fast Company, Fortune* and many other magazines fill their pages with stories about real people, with strong messages that can be helpful to you.

Change your organization's main newsletter and staff meetings to include at least one story about the people who make your organization successful.

Don't focus on the executives; focus on the people who really make things happen—the employees and the customers. Share their hopes and dreams, their hobbies, and their favorite books. You'll be surprised to find those stories will be the most shared through your organization.

Commandment #5:
Be Visual

One picture is worth a thousand words.
—Fred A. Bernard

WE LIVE IN A VISUAL WORLD. From etchings on cave walls to television, visuals have commanded attention for millions of years. We learned this lesson in kindergarten through "show and tell." Five-year-old minds simply can't choose the right words. So the visual elements of props and pictures help focus the communication energy and create a multisensory experience.

Most audiences today have attention spans similar to that of a kindergartner. Even in one-on-one conversations, a listener's attention may fade quickly if you, the presenter, are not immediately animated and compelling. Show and tell engages the mind of the audience, and projects a confidence from the presenter that the audience can feel. It's one of the oldest, best tricks in the book.

Why, then, do so many well-intentioned leaders try the black-ink-on-white-paper method first? Bullet-point memos and letters are poor techniques to build consensus, launch a new project, or run an important meeting. You know exactly what I mean. Every day, smart professionals sit around conference tables studying black ink on white paper. If the subject isn't exceptionally exciting or critically alarming, the mind starts to wander. Time and energy are wasted. Are you preparing one of those black-ink-on-white-paper presentations today? If so, stop and think: *What makes you wake from that wandering gaze during Sunday morning sermons to instantly pay special attention to the pulpit? What holds your attention in meetings? What technique did that excellent presenter use to focus everyone's attention on the same thing?*

It was a visual in one of three forms:

- An animated delivery style where the *presenter himself or herself* was a visual;
- Show and tell using something physical to look at (a prop); or
- Word pictures that brought the language to life in your mind.

Leaders who understand the power of visuals turn ordinary conversations into television programs inside the audience's head.

Making Yourself Visual

The first step is to recognize that you, *yourself,* are visual. You don't need Paul Newman's blue eyes or Julia Robert's smile to be effective. Just standing at the end of the table is more interesting than sitting in the middle. When you write key points in colored markers on a flip chart, you are far more interesting than when you read the bullet points from a memo. When you show a design sketch, poster board, or product samples from the line, you are much more captivating than when you describe it with words alone. And like many of those tellers of famous "fish stories," you are much more engaging when you talk with your hands. Excellent leaders use their hands to demonstrate highs and lows, peaks and valleys, and points they really want to drive home. The bolder the gesture the better. Think of how much more fun it is to "show" the difference between a "minnow" and a "monster" in a friendly fishing contest. Especially if you caught the monster!

Visual Anchors

One of the simplest ways to become a visual communicator is to draw. Simple stick figures and geometric shapes can be terrific communication tools. The drawings serve as visual "anchors" to establish a concept firmly in the mind. Even if the nitty-gritty details can't be recalled, the visual helps people remember your message. Ironically, some of the best one-on-one-communicators I know are accountants and engineers. Their personalities don't necessarily accommodate presenting to big crowds, but one-on-one, they can be wonderful because they love to *draw pictures*. Drawing helps them talk, share, listen—communicate.

And from the listener end of the equation, it's much easier to pay attention to finance and process discussions with graphs and charts that jump to life at the tip of a pencil. It's easier to comprehend a rising trend line for expenses and a receding revenue line when the lines are actually drawn. And it's much easier to discuss critical dates and milestones when they are anchored by colored marks on a timeline.

Russ Michaletz, a partner in the tax division of Arthur Andersen, is an excellent example. Russ carries the advantage (or burden) of being both a certified public accountant (CPA) and a lawyer. His success is directly tied to how well people understand very complex tax situations. Without sharp communication skills, he could bore people to tears! When Russ talks business, he has the pen out immediately. "I just have to draw concepts in models," he explained. "I spend most of my time on two activities: Creating solutions to complex problems and teaching other people to understand those solutions. It really helps to get things out of my head and on paper so we can all work together."

Below is one of his drawings. Russ is no Picasso, but the point of his drawing is simple: There must be an equal balance of benefit from the three parties.

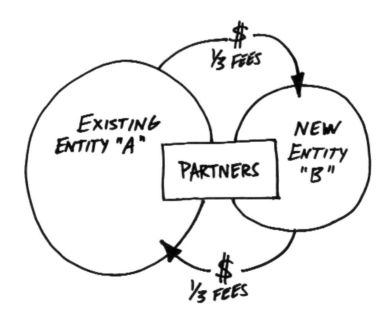

Picassos Not Needed

Ted Contag, a financial executive with Aid Association for Lutherans (AAL), has learned through experience the difficulties of discussing the subtle differences of financial products. His clients look to him for help in navigating the complexities of hundreds of financial products. To help, Ted has developed the drawing below to describe the features and benefits of Variable Universal Life Insurance.

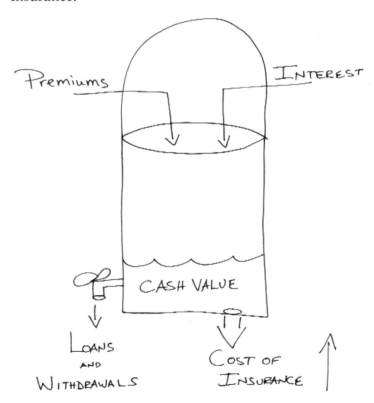

He begins by drawing the outline of the bucket, with a wavy "water line" near the bottom of the bucket. The water represents "your money" in premiums paid in, and interest earned from the investment. The more payments in and the better the investments, the faster the water level rises. The spigot on the side of the bucket represents a special feature: When the investor needs extra cash immediately, the bucket can be tapped, and water (money) can be used.

"I can't tell you how hard it was to explain the Variable Universal Life product to people before I developed the bucket drawing," Ted said. "I tried lots of different stories, constantly tripping over the right sequence and the right approach. It doesn't really matter that I'm a lousy artist—it really helps to draw it. Now I concentrate on letting the act of building the bucket in front of my clients tell the story of how Variable Universal Life products can give them a decent investment with exceptional flexibility."

Drawing works wonders in one-on-one and group settings. Napkins, notebooks, overhead projectors, whiteboards, blackboards, and flip charts are the visual communicator's canvas. White paper tablecloths in restaurants are terrific for communicating. You can make lists, draw graphical models, and make mathematical calculations with your pen or the kids' meal crayons.

Beware of Death by PowerPoint

PowerPoint is an excellent organizational tool for presentations. And when used correctly, it helps make ideas and concepts come to life by making them visual. However, PowerPoint presentations have probably killed more brain cells than the use of controlled substances. You know the drill. First, the presenter turns on the LCD projector, then turns off the lights, and reads every slide word for word—and usually the slides are packed full of words. Your mind turns to mush. The presenter has just committed death by PowerPoint.

PowerPoint lulls leaders into thinking that the slide show *is* the presentation—and they pack everything into it, making it become the center of focus instead of the presenter. Herein lies the mistake. PowerPoint should only be used as a visual aid. No amount of flying bullet points or clip art graphics can resurrect a crappy presentation. In fact, it has a better chance of ruining good content than helping describe and promote it when it's used poorly.

Leaders at the Pentagon learned this the hard way. *The Wall Street Journal* reported on the military's decreasing effectiveness in persuading members of Congress to fund top priorities. In the article, congressional veterans recalled the days when generals would march onto the Senate floor with seven poster boards describing the situation, strategy, and tactical plans. The final poster board was a budget. The average presentation lasted approximately 16 minutes, including questions. Most programs were funded with little resistance.

When the brain wizards at the Pentagon discovered PowerPoint, the presentations averaged 57 slides, took more than an hour, and seldom were funded. More often than not, the senators requested more research and more detail before they could make a funding decision. The article concluded by pointing out that Pentagon officials had finally discovered that they were numbing the minds of the people they were trying to impress, and killing their chances for funding. Today they are using poster boards again.

Your best chances for success are to think of your visual communication as a "multimedia" experience. Use props to demonstrate your points, talk with your hands, draw on flip charts and white boards, and use PowerPoint only to guide and illustrate the discussion.

Developing a Show-and-Tell Style

Even the simplest show-and-tell concepts can electrify a conversation. When Jim Clifford was the president and CEO of Firstar Bank Minnesota, he learned this lesson well. In a charitable moment, he volunteered to explain how the U.S. economy works to a group of high school economics students. "I was a total failure," he recalled. "I didn't know my audience very well, and I had nothing interesting to show them. They were bored stiff and I wasn't having any fun." That humbling experience motivated him to invent a clever show-and-tell technique.

Using Props

In the mid-1990s, the bank's ad firm ran a series of very successful television advertisements. The ads showed mountains of cash being moved around in the vault by a front-end loader. People easily got the message that the bank was eager to loan cash. The genesis of Jim's show-and-tell idea came from the boxes and boxes of fake money left over from when the commercials were filmed. Now he's eager to teach with his show-and-tell game. In the center of a table, he dumps a big pile of fake money.

"I appoint the person immediately to my right as Bill Gates," he explained. "One third of the money is moved to a pile called 'The Government.' Another third goes in 'The Bank' for savings, and I give the final third to 'Bill' for spending. Of course 'Bill' is filthy rich, but he needs to spend his money for all the things in life that people require. So, I ask 'Bill' to take one-third of his money and give it to 'The Government' and another one-third to 'The Bank.' The next person does the same thing, and so on. It doesn't take very long to see the relationship between the three most powerful elements of the economy: taxes, investment, and spending."

Since inventing this show-and-tell technique, Jim is excited about teaching the inner workings of the U.S. economy. Everyone enjoys it—students, clients, and employees.

Stretching the Truth

The partners in a large professional services firm were huddled around a conference table concerned about a downturn in business. They were heatedly engaged in conversation about how to generate more business. One of the quietest leaders reached into his pocket, retrieved a thick rubber band, and began to speak.

"One of the strengths of this firm is our ability to be flexible," he said. With these words he began to stretch the rubber band. Left to right. Up and down. The action commanded attention. He continued, "We accept many different types of assignments, looking for big, long-term client relationships. And the deeper we get into our client's organization, the more we can help. And the more we help them, the busier we get." With each sentence he began to stretch the rubber band farther and farther. When he was ready to make his point, he held the rubber band at eye level and stretched it out from left to right as far as it would allow.

"While the rest of the company is pretty soft, the people on the manufacturing team are absolutely stretched to the limits. The junior staff is consistently working 30 percent over capacity, week after week. If this continues, we're going to make mistakes, under deliver, and jeopardize our firm's largest client." By now, the partners were fixated on that rubber band. Was it going to snap and hit him in the face? Before he finished and put the rubber band on the table, the tension it had created emphasized his point more than just words. A little dramatic? Yes. But memorable.

Salt-and-Pepper Decision-Making

Leadership communication often involves solving problems. And most of the time, problems have more than one solution. Our instincts tell us to deliver options in threes: Father, Son, and Holy Ghost. Ready, set, go! Peter, Paul, and Mary. But problem solving is easier when you whittle your choices down to two options that can be polarized: Either one choice or the other. I like to use the salt and pepper shakers in restaurants to clarify difficult conversations. The conversation sounds like this: "Let's try to make a decision. I can see many options, but let's whittle them down to two choices. The salt shaker represents choice number one, and the pepper shaker represents choice number two. We can't have both."

As the conversation intensifies, all of the energy is channeled into two inanimate objects. Nine times out of ten, the salt and pepper shakers are picked up, rotated, dragged across the table—and sometimes even switch sides! But ultimately, the visual representation speeds up the process and helps drive people to a solution.

Back to those restaurants with paper tablecloths— you can write and use objects to help illustrate your point. If the restaurant has crayons, you can draw your graphs and stick figures in multiple colors! When you're done, you can tear off your scribbling (pasta sauce and all) and take it back to the office for immediate recall.

Using Vivid Language

My children love to play "20 Questions." As urbanites, we've learned to fill our idle time in the minivan by playing games that engage the mind. You know the game: One person has the responsibility to think of an object. The others are allowed to ask only 20 questions to discover the identity of the object. Only questions that can be answered with yes or no are allowed.

Very early, the kids discovered that one of the most strategic questions for this game was "Is it bigger than a bread box?" Why? Because the answer creates a word picture that shapes the entire game. No one really knows the exact size of a "bread box." But the suggestion, "No, it's smaller than a bread box," immediately brings everyone into the same general frame of reference. Oh, if all leadership communication endeavors were so simple.

OK, I realize the grammar aficionados are cringing right now. Some of what I call "word pictures" are really metaphors and similes. However, I understand my audience pretty well. No one would listen to me if I told them they needed to incorporate more similes into their communication. Here are a few specific word pictures used by leaders I respect:

- . . . let's look at this situation from 50,000 feet.
- . . . let's just put a stake in the ground and start.
- . . . let's start to see the pink flags before we run into red flags.
- . . . we need to provide a smorgasbord of options.
- . . . as broad and consistent as the Clinique counter at Nordstrom's.
- . . . don't look at a problem as a frog you have to swallow.
- . . . service as consistent as McDonald's, and authentic as a Coke.
- . . . don't just plug holes in the dike, get upstream.
- . . . we can't be hunting elephants with a BB gun.

Word pictures are important in written and spoken communication. Mark Peterson, president and CEO of Lutheran Social Service of Minnesota, crafted this compelling report with excellent word pictures.

Lutheran Social Service of Minnesota
PRESIDENT'S REPORT

SEPTEMBER, 2000

> *The Devil Track River is a rocky, sometimes raging, sometimes nearly dry North Shore trout stream. It finds its way into Lake Superior just east of Grand Marais. Like a lot of north shore streams, it harbors brook trout, most of which are*

not noteworthy—except for their astonishing coloration and succulent flavor. A fishing guide confided that there was a particular stretch of the stream, however, that held heftier brook trout and was seldom fished. A few days later, I was there.

Fishing the Devil Track isn't easy. There are no trails at streamside. The streambed is jagged rock of small and huge proportion. There's little straight about the water's course. Pools appear without warning. In late summer there are stretches of low, unfishable water. Bushes and tree branches overhang the stream where the best fishing is.

Generally in streams like this, smaller fish are voracious eaters of insects that are on the stream's surface. Larger fish hunker down in the bottom of pools, eating what sweeps past them on the edge of the current. It's easier, splashier, in some ways more spectacular to fish on the surface. When a fish strikes, it's pretty obvious. Different skill is required to plumb the depths of the short, abrupt pools of the Devil Track.

Interpreting Mission for the New Millennium . . . will take us on journeys like the Devil Track. The path we've laid out is seldom taken. Indeed, in some ways we will be creating the path. We will need to listen carefully to all manner of guides. It will be tough work. We believe there are grand prizes of service for us, but seizing them will require considerable fortitude and skill. We will need to be persistent and focused in our quest for *the larger prizes. We will also need to be prepared for hidden challenges.*

I do believe, deeply, that the long-range plan has started us on a most important journey, one for which we are well prepared. Even at this writing, the plan has begun to re-shape LSS. Evidence of that is found in the accompanying management reports.

There was more to the report—mostly housekeeping items. But I think you'll agree, this isn't the typical report from a president. The constituents noticed. "Tales of the Devil Track River" opened a fresh perspective on the intensity of the challenges facing LSS. And, it piqued a curiosity in fly-fishing for many.

Mark could have chosen typical methods to write about the future of LSS. Stop, go back, and read the letter again and contemplate how you could insert more vivid language into your communication.

Commandment #5
Practical Tactical Tips

Try these practical tactical tips to help you apply *Commandment #5: Be Visual,* to your leadership:

Learn to use flip charts.

Write your next meeting agenda in bullet points on a flip chart instead of passing out the typical memo. Take notes from the conversation on the flip chart so everyone can see your thinking. To get used to the concept, buy the game "Pictionary," and play it with your management team on flip charts.

Give multimedia presentations.

Stand up for presentations, use PowerPoint to introduce and guide the discussion, draw your concepts on a flip chart, and use props—real, three-dimensional objects—to demonstrate your point. Show the books and magazines you use for reference, mount important graphics on poster board, and use your hands for emphasis.

Develop visual models for your management concepts.

Use circles, squares, triangles, and stick figures to bring your messages to life. Draw on whatever you have available—napkins, tablecloths, flip charts, whiteboards, notepads, or overheads.

Commandment #6:
Practice No Surprises

It's amazing . . . with all of the outstanding medical technology advancements, people still can't read your mind.

—David Ness, Vice President, Medtronic, and past chair, American Heart Association

EVER HEARD THAT NO NEWS IS GOOD NEWS? I don't buy it. With all of the innovative ways to stay in touch with people, no news is neutral at best. In the information age, people expect to have immediate access to the information they need to run their lives. And in the absence of information, they will assume the negative. As a leader today, you absolutely must keep people informed.

Practice no surprises is a 360-degree concept—a never-ending cycle of "heads up" and "close the loop" two-way communication. "Heads up" is a forecasting strategy; "close the loop" is a follow-through strategy. Both are equally important, as information itself becomes a tool for how well people around you execute. Today's most talented leaders understand that one of the drivers of high-functioning teams is the constant flow of information. The leader's job is to paint a clear picture of success and then create an environment where people have the tools and information they need to succeed.

This is especially true in environments built on constant change. Information helps people stay grounded and less threatened. Visit Chicago and you'll notice a seven-minute weather report on the evening news and the saying goes: "If you don't like the weather, blink twice and it will change." Visit Hawaii and you won't even get a weather forecast because the weather hardly ever changes. In climates of constant change, people really do care about the report of what happened today (closing the loop) and what is expected tomorrow (heads up).

We can translate the weather report into everyday actions. Team members are more likely to be prepared and engaged in new activities if they know what's coming. Do you do a good job of forecasting impending meetings or special projects? Do you give people a heads up when you foresee changes that will affect their work? And, on the flip side, do you close the loop with timely praise when you see a job well done? When things happen to an organization that seem to catch it by surprise, people get rattled. They wonder . . . who's keeping watch, anyway? A continual cycle of heads up and close the loop is the bedrock of *practice no surprises*—the blocking and tackling that makes excellent leadership possible.

The Value of "Over-Communicating"

John Goodrich left a high-paying corporate job running a $120 million division to pursue a dream of leadership in the start-up high-tech arena. Today he is CEO of Infrared Systems, Inc., a technology company that designs and manufactures low-cost infrared cameras for industrial and public safety applications. Soon after he accepted the challenge, the basic technology in the flagship product failed. The company nearly went bankrupt twice. He explained:

> *I quickly learned that the corporate and start-up worlds were light years apart. Within weeks of starting my new job, I was worrying about how we were going to meet payroll. Our technology was very exciting, but still fragile—engineering needed my support, but I had to spend most of my time trying to raise money to keep us alive. I was constantly torn between the big picture and the hourly details. Success ultimately depends on how well the people around you execute. They need to be engaged with the mission and focused on the right things. The most valuable lesson I learned is that, in times of rapid, constant change, you need to over communicate. The more change that was forced upon us, the more we needed to tell each other what was going on. In the toughest times at ISI, we were making significant changes every day. Changes in the technology, in our people, in our fundamental processes. We couldn't afford surprises.*

Making People Feel Good

John used another version of *practice no surprises* to help him rebuild. "I honestly believe that you have to go out of your way to make people feel good about themselves," he explained. "That means catching them in the middle of something that is positive and closing the loop with immediate praise. And when we started making money, I knew I had to do something to show appreciation for the extraordinary efforts that kept the company alive." He called an impromptu company meeting and told them he was proud of each and every one of them.

> *I told the story of how this company was started, and how surviving our setbacks was a tremendous accomplishment. But I didn't stop there. First, we gave everyone stock options in the company. We didn't lure people with the promise of getting rich, but we decided to reward people with that promise. Then, I had a one-on-one meeting with every single person in the company to thank them for their contributions. I shared salary information I had found for similar companies, and promised everyone that I'd get them to a better-than-average salary level if we continued to climb toward our goals. I told them I intended to pay above average, but the company also expected above-average productivity. And in exchange, we agreed to be totally open and honest with each other. That's how we operated while trying to stay alive, and that's the same way we needed to operate going forward.*

Learning the Hard Way

Staying totally open and honest isn't always easy. John recalled a poignant moment from his corporate days that crystallized the need for open communication with direct reports. "I had a very talented, driven person reporting to me when the company was about $50M. At our annual review, we discussed something that I was particularly disappointed about regarding this employee's performance. It was a really tough moment for me, but even tougher on the other end. As it turns out, I learned an extremely important lesson about feedback.

"My direct report looked me straight in the eye and said: 'This is totally unfair, and unprofessional. You've never even mentioned this to me before. I had no idea you expected that from me—we've never discussed it. A performance review is no place for surprises. Your job as my leader is to make sure there aren't any surprises in performance reviews. You've let me down.' He was right. I had been thinking about my dissatisfaction for quite some time. I was wrong. I apologized, but never forgot that message."

People Can't Read Your Mind

David Ness, whom we met in Commandment #1, learned to overcome his quiet, reserved, Scandinavian tendencies to lead the American Heart Association (AHA) through a pivotal time. He entered his position as chairman of the board for the AHA at a time when the organization was strong, but not necessarily thriving. "I think too often organizations forget why they exist," David explained. "And I think we could have. Our mission is to reduce death and disability from heart disease and stroke. As I accepted the role of chair, I began asking some questions in my own mind: *Are we being the best stewards of our resources—$350 million and 4.3 million volunteers?*

Heart disease is the number-one disabler of Americans—I needed to know the answer."

David engaged the people around him in the discussion, asking the tough questions and building the answers together. They discovered they were working as an information *distribution* company, but at the core, they were really an information *generation* company, providing highly credible information with breakthrough research. The reality of that discovery meant significant changes that threatened many people.

As the board chair, and the driver of this change, I didn't want people to try and read my mind. We wanted to create change the right way. So, involvement of the broad constituency was absolutely critical. We wanted open communication and involvement to be at the core of our decision-making process. There was a whole series of meetings with the people who would be directly affected by these changes. We had groups of 200-plus people working on different potential, strategic, driving-force applications ultimately asking: "What are the tasks that we have to do really well in order to accomplish our mission?" Through it all we had huge meetings, some of which were fraught with all kinds of angst. But we allowed people to share their issues. Ultimately, even after we changed the role of a lot of important people in the organization, we had raised the most money on a percentage basis than we had in the past 15 years. I'm proud to say—in a very non-Scandinavian way—that the American Heart

Association is arguably the strongest not-for-profit in the healthcare arena today. And we did it together.

The more people that are involved and the higher the stakes, the more important *practice no surprises* becomes. People have their own frames of reference, their own set of expectations, and often the simplest things get out of whack. For example, two major metropolitan healthcare corporations engaged in a joint venture were in negotiations about their future. The boards were filled with prominent, highly respected people. After months of discussing common principles and values, very little had been accomplished. There was no progress to report to either set of shareholders. The negotiations were stalled because one organization was assuming that both parties wanted to continue in the hospital business.

At the height of the puzzling impasse, someone asked members of one board the most basic question that had never been asked: "Do you want to be in the hospital business or not?" To the astonishment of the questioner, the answer was no, with all the board members nodding in complete agreement. Suddenly the events of the past year made sense. Why hadn't someone spoken up sooner? Why did one organization expect the other to read its minds? We'll probably never know. But the waste of time and emotional energy in good-faith negotiations diverted everyone from the purpose at hand—to serve people in need.

I've never heard anyone say, "Our leader is communicating too much . . . providing too much good information." It's actually quite the opposite. I've met leaders who believe that a quarterly printed newsletter sent to employees or posted on a bulletin board keeps their organization well-informed. I've met several who've said, "My door's always open. If they want more information, they can just come in and ask." That's an antiquated attitude, and those leaders are failing. They haven't grasped the power in the phrase that pays: *If people don't understand you, it's your problem.*

Making Client Satisfaction a Passion

Lynn Casey's passion is client satisfaction. As CEO of Padilla Speer Beardsley Public Relations, it permeates everything she does. And that enthusiasm sets a terrific example for the people important to her success. She has had a broad range of experiences in her career, and her *vita* is filled with client success stories. "Clients need to know you will be there when they need you," she said. "And above all, if you make a promise, keep it."

This is brought to life through a client-management tool Lynn developed called the "Getting Started Meeting." Every new client is treated to a Getting Started Meeting, where all aspects of account relationships are discussed. Together, everyone reviews the goals and individual roles in achieving those goals. Everyone shares communication expectations—whether or not it's okay to call someone at home, preferences for e-mail versus fax versus phone, and what's a basic standard for a reasonable response time—from both parties. There's even a section in the meeting to talk about passions and pet peeves. What Lynn has done is intentionally build *practice no surprises* into a formal meeting. It's not surprising to know that her company has client retention rates far beyond the national norm.

It deserves to be said that *Commandment #2: Understand Your Audience,* applies directly in the application of *practice no surprises.* If the people important to your success are doers, you'll drive them crazy, and perhaps do more harm than good by sending long, arduous "just closing the loop" messages. Some people need more detail than others. Some people respond better to voice-mail, some to e-mail, and some to face-to-face communication. Use your sensibilities to forecast and follow through, but by all means, *practice no surprises.* The people important to your success will notice, and appreciate your leadership.

Commandment #6
Practical Tactical Tips

Try these practical tactical tips to help you apply *Commandment # 6: Practice No Surprises,* to your leadership:

Summarize in meetings, and ask to make sure you have understanding.

Write down the promises made, and the promises kept. Keeping an accurate record will help you create an internal expectation of accountability, and help you move things forward.

As you plan ahead, close the loop on what's been done.

Tell the people important to your success what's

been done, and what's left to be done. Voicemail and e-mail are terrific for sending messages like this: *"Met with Mary on Friday as promised. She had terrific feedback, and will help us find people for the focus group. We'll talk more about this at the Tuesday staff meeting."*

Send e-mails or memos ahead of time about what you intend to cover in meetings.

When people are prepared and ready to contribute, the increase in productivity will be worth the extra effort.

BONUS

Reward people when you catch them in the act of doing something terrific. Don't wait until "the right time." If you want to publicly recognize someone later, that's fine. But don't miss the opportunity to immediately close the loop and make someone feel good about themselves.

Commandment #7:
Put It on Paper

My experience is that people don't hear what you are trying to say, so you need to write it down for them.
> —Dick Kovacevich, CEO, Wells Fargo & Company

THE MOST DRAMATIC MOMENTS IN THE HIT TELEVISION DRAMA *NYPD BLUE* HAPPEN IN THE "COFFEE ROOM," where suspects are questioned and allowed to explain themselves. Everyone has a compelling story. But it's fascinating how those stories evolve and change, morphing as the situation around them changes. When Detective Sipowitz is ready for business, he slaps a yellow legal pad and pencil on the table and says, "Write that down and we'll see what we can do." There's real power in putting things on paper. It helps create commitment.

The people who invented the Franklin Planner® understand this commandment well. Franklin Planner devotees run their lives by writing things down—in the proper place. It helps them stay focused. But *put it on paper* isn't about "fessing up" to crimes or becoming a better time manager. It's about articulating expectations, keeping promises, and creating focus.

The overused sports metaphor "we've got to have every player on the same page" is appropriate in two ways. First, it implies that the information about how the team is going to function has been *written down* in the playbook. Second, the team won't successfully execute if everyone is reading from a different page in the playbook. This seems so obvious, yet misunderstandings and poor execution are commonplace, fueled by poorly articulated plays in the playbook or, worse yet, having no playbooks at all.

Excellent leaders know putting values, visions, and intentions to paper helps create focus. It allows for efficiency, collaboration, and collective improvement. This is particularly important in a culture that is increasingly casual and cynical about promises. Throwaway lines like "I'll call you and we'll do lunch," "you'll have it tomorrow," or the infamous "the check's in the mail," are all too commonplace. A cycle of broken promises, no matter how small, erodes the integrity of the leader and the culture that the leader is trying to create.

Taking the time to follow up, recap conversations (and promises) in an e-mail or memo, and then following through is critical. You can build credibility with simple statements like: "As promised, I'm sending you a copy of that article I mentioned when we met. I think you'll find the paragraph on page two especially relevant. Call me if you'd like to discuss it further."

Everyone knows writing can be intimidating. Most of us have vivid memories of school papers "corrected" with a red pen. Seeing that red ink just made you cringe. And what if people don't like what you have to say? But if we can face down our intimidation and put what we have to say on paper so people can study the words, it is much easier to handle criticism from peers and employees. Leadership requires clarity, and putting your thoughts on paper helps create clarity. The best practice, if you do not enjoy writing, is to throw your thoughts on paper and enlist the help of the people around you who do enjoy writing. Together you can articulate the thoughts, goals, and deeds that are important to your success.

Beware the Power of the Pen

Wasn't it Confucius who said: "The sword cuts both ways?" Anything you put on paper can be saved and recalled at any time. And that's not always good. Early in my career, I wrote a stream-of-consciousness document, venting my frustrations regarding a specific employee. Cutting thoughts, piercing words. It helped clear my mind. Once I reached the cleansing point, I decided to delete the document. The next morning I arrived at the office only to discover that somehow, through the magic of technology, I had accidentally printed it, and the employee read it. We were both devastated. Although we talked it through, the damage was never fully repaired.

This brings to mind an important rule of thumb: *If it's good, write it down; if it's bad, air it out.* I should have had the courage to "air it out"—talk those frustrations through in person. We both agreed to throw away the paper, but those cutting words will never be forgotten.

You can harness that power and use it for building something special. Take the time to articulate your thoughts and intentions on paper and share them. When you *deliver on those words*, you create an environment of accountability and respect that will endure.

Putting It on Paper for Wells Fargo

When Norwest Corporation and Wells Fargo joined forces to create one of the largest financial services organizations in the world, Dick Kovacevich knew exactly what to do. He'd been in this situation before. Several years earlier, he'd arrived at Norwest from Citicorp, and soon after was named CEO of Norwest. "The CEO's main responsibility is to identify, define, and articulate the culture," he explained. At Norwest—and now at Wells Fargo—that articulation takes the form of a pocket-sized brochure called *Visions and Values*. The most current version for the combined Wells Fargo entity reflects the evolution of the document from the early days at Norwest. "It's important to understand that the *Visions and Values* booklet wasn't written as a public relations tool. It was intended, and still is intended today, to be a living document for establishing the values we think are important for our success. When we wrote *Visions and Values* for the new Wells Fargo, it was my job to describe our collective thoughts—it's critical that it reflected our combined cultures, not mine alone."

Here's how the *Visions and Values for the New Wells Fargo* begins:

The Journey: Going from Good to Great

This is about you and our brand new company. It's about where we've come from, where we're headed, and how we're going to get there. We're all proud of the organizations we've come from. We're all proud of our accomplishments, and rightly so. The old Norwest was a great company. The old Wells Fargo was a great company. So were the more than 1,500 banks and financial services companies that have become a part of our company the past 150 years. The merger of equals—Norwest and Wells Fargo—however, did not automatically create a great company. So far, we're probably only "good." Who wants to settle for "good"?

Where We're Headed: Our Vision

*So, this is about our vision for going from "good" to "great." In many ways, we're starting over. We have to prove ourselves all over again—to ourselves, our customers, our communities, and our stockholders. This is not a task. This is a journey. Just like the journeys our predecessors embarked on in the early years of Norwest and Wells Fargo. Every journey has a destination. To get to that destination, you need a vision. Ours is an ambitious one. **We want to satisfy all of our customer's financial needs and help them succeed financially.***

The next 30 pages include discussions of concepts such as:

- How do we picture success?
- What is the new Wells Fargo?
- How do we make money?
- What are our 10 strategic initiatives?
- What are our values?

"I'm much more of a written communicator than a verbal communicator," Dick admitted. "My experience has been that most people don't hear what you are trying to say, so you need to write it down for them." Ask most Wells Fargo employees and they'll either be carrying their copy of *Visions and Values* on them, or their copy will be within arm's reach. Wells Fargo's vision and values work because Kovacevich wrote them down, and he never quits repeating what he wrote. Every time he speaks, he mentions *Vision and Values*. And it trickles down into everyday interactions.

Guiding Principles Spark Knowledge Sharing

Throughout the 40-year history of steady growth, the workforce at Padilla Speer Beardsley Public Relations had been stable. Most of the employees learned the values by hanging around a long time. But a three-year period of explosive growth in the late 1990s created a need to bring people together—to preserve the culture the firm was founded upon. The chairman, John Beardsley, articulated these guiding principles:

- Always tell the truth.
- Work from a body of knowledge.
- Respect the abilities of colleagues and associates.
- Be fiscally prudent.
- Be adventurous.
- Lead clients, don't follow.
- Strive for excellence.

At first glance, they seem almost too simple. But the magic was in *sharing them*. Within weeks, the employee-owners created regular opportunities to discuss the guiding principles. Now that the values were articulated, people were craving discussion. Staffers began sharing client stories at company-wide meetings about how they integrated the guiding principles into their work. And, the firm incorporated "Work from a body of knowledge" and "Lead clients, don't follow" into its marketing strategy to create a point of difference. Before the guiding principles were articulated in writing, they were virtually impossible to discuss, and difficult to put into action.

Communicating the Need for Integrity

Everyone knows people in the healthcare industry are hypersensitive about moral, ethical, and legal compliance issues. And they should be. So, how does a leader in the medical device industry create a common sense of integrity among the more than 28,000 employees doing business in 127 countries across the globe? Bill George, who we met in Commandment #4, believes sharing the basic values that guide the work of Medtronic is the best way to keep its endeavors on the straight and narrow. That's why he created the Medtronic Compliance Program. The backbone of the program is a carefully worded document that declares, "All employees of Medtronic and its subsidiaries worldwide must adhere to Medtronic's policies—without exception. Medtronic's values and conduct must be generally consistent throughout the world while recognizing the cultural diversity of our global presence."

Every employee reviews the Medtronic Compliance information annually with a facilitator, and each person is required to sign the document. The underlying principle is the same as the one used by Detective Sipowitz in *NYPD Blues*. Discussing and learning about the values and compliance issues is one thing. Signing the document is another. Employees who are confronted with the failure to live up to the standards of the Medtronic Compliance Program face immediate disciplinary action, including termination. That's because an organization like Medtronic cannot afford integrity to be optional.

Why CEOs Fail

"Every leader feels a deep sense of purpose to make good for the people in their organization," remarked Paul Harmel, who we met in Commandment #4. "At Lifetouch, we have an awesome responsibility to preserve precious memories for families," Paul explained. "We have partnerships with the thousands of teachers, principals, and PTA groups across the U. S. and Canada. It's an emotional business—people absolutely love portraits of their family members, but they get really upset if we fail them." As he was settling into the role of CEO, Paul became fascinated with a *Fortune* magazine article, "Why CEOs Fail."

"It might seem totally obvious," he laughed, "but the main reason CEOs—or any leader for that matter—fail, is because of poor execution. There are thousands of companies that have failed with terrific business plans. They simply couldn't execute those terrific plans. Something about the leadership didn't communicate the expectations clearly and keep people focused on accomplishing the plan."

You won't find a computer on Paul's desk. He's a product of a different era of executive development. He's a hands-on CEO, committed to keeping people on task. "I spend the majority of my time making sure people understand our expectations. You give me the choice of investing in a company with a mediocre business plan that's executed to perfection, and a company that has the best plan in the world with poor execution—I'll take perfect execution any day," he said. "I believe most leaders have a really tough time holding people accountable. People get too wrapped up in circumstantial things. At the end of the day, you have to be able to put down on paper what is being accomplished, and measure that against your goals and objectives. The most disrespectful thing you can do is to not be honest with your people. When you put it down on paper, it's much easier."

Battle of the Highest Bidder

Nowhere is this commandment, *put it on paper,* more important than in the retention of good people. Beverly Kaye, a Los Angeles-based retention consultant, was quoted in *The Wall Street Journal* offering simple but sound advice: "If you think money is the only way to retain people, you've lost the battle," she wrote. "There is always a higher bidder. In competitive situations every manager should sit down with their people for a closed-door, one-on-one meeting focused on the question: 'You're really important to us, so what can we do to keep you?' Then take notes, and produce your answers in writing. Putting it in writing shows you listened. Putting it in writing demonstrates a promise that you'll do what you can to make sure people are happy."

Commandment #7
Practical Tactical Tips

Try these practical tactical tips to help you apply *Commandment #7: Put It on Paper,* to your leadership:

Memorize this rule of thumb: Good news, write it down; bad news, air it out.

Whatever you write down on paper can be saved and recalled forever. That's why you should never write a seething e-mail or letter—it could very easily come back to haunt you. Put your positive thoughts in writing, and talk through your frustrations.

Make sure a recap memo is written for every meeting you attend where people have accepted responsibility to carry something forward.

It's one of the simplest—and most effective—tools to implement, but few people take the time to do it. Then use the recap memo to prepare for future meetings, and to hold people accountable (including yourself).

Hand-write thank-you notes, address the envelope by hand, stamp the envelope, and send it through the U.S. Postal Service to really make an impression.

E-mail is not the same as a hand-written note. E-mail is too easy to have the same impact and it's not very private.

Commandment #8:
Be Careful What You Call Things

> Most people . . . are much more inclined to
> accept the first story they hear.
> —Thucydides, 400 BC

WE ALL KNOW FIRST IMPRESSIONS ARE POWERFUL. With
interpersonal communications, the first impression is
often visual—how you look and act. But with the
increasing use of e-mail, the words you choose are
critical to first impressions. As a leader, you have the
opportunity to shape the frame of reference for
people about challenges and opportunities. Well-
selected words can engage the mind in powerful
ways.

Ancient scholar Thucydides said in 400 BC:
*"Most people . . . are much more inclined to accept
the first story they hear."* This underscores the importance of "framing," and it illustrates how important
the intentional use of language is to human interaction. More than 2400 years later, that same advice is
still being repeated in business journals. As recently
as 1998, the *Harvard Business Review* restated
Thucydides: "When considering a decision, the mind

gives disproportionate weight to the first information it receives. Initial impressions, estimates or data 'anchor' subsequent thoughts and judgments."

Choosing the Right Words

Choosing your language carefully will help you soothe tension in times of concern, and spark change with less resistance. Of course, wordsmithing, or spin doctoring has given PR people, corporate leaders, and politicians alike a bad reputation. Labels like "right-sizing" used in place of "layoffs," and phrases like "we don't have problems, just opportunities to improve," have created a population of cynics. "Dilbert" fans snicker over the abundance of acronyms and double-speak. Arguments can be made that in these complicated times, things need to be called exactly what they are: Budget cuts are budget cuts, not "situational adjustments." However cynical you might be about "corporate speak," you'll inspire action more quickly if you think more about the words you choose, and be intentional about what you call things.

It's a Store

The word *stores* will anchor the Kovacevich legacy in the financial services industry. In the mid-90s, Dick urged analysts to stop thinking of banks in terms of net assets, but in terms of sales-per-square-foot retail "stores." It signaled a change from "institutional thinking" to "retail thinking." He argued that people today really go to banks to "buy things." Target and the Gap are evaluated on sales-per-square-foot; so too should banks. This was revolutionary thinking, and it caught some people by surprise.

"The whole concept of a 'branch,' 'location,' or 'office' is flawed thinking because it makes it seem like it's not as good as the main office," Dick explained. "Especially when all the research shows that people generally think of banks as being cold and arrogant, or like a mausoleum with stone pillars. The use of the word *store* makes people think of a pleasant, exciting place where people want to buy things. And that's what I want our customers to think about.

"It was difficult for many of our people to handle at first—some thought it made banking sound cheap. But we got people to examine what we really do. It sparked a lot of conversation about service, customer satisfaction, the hours of the week we were available for our customers and much more. Today, we have thousands of Wells Fargo stores spread all around the country. And our customer retention reflects our customer service mentality."

Being Fully Present

Like Kovacevich, Bill George created a big change with a simple thought. "Since Medtronic is in the medical device business, we ought to be so good at the concept of health that our customers are going to want to emulate us," he explained. "Not for our products, but for how we live our lives." He challenged his people to develop a program to ensure all Medtronic employees would be *fully present* on the job.

"When Bill George challenged me with the thought of being *fully present,* it really made me think," recalled

David Ness. "You're *fully present* if you are focusing all your talent and energy on what's important—and that's serving the customer. How can you be fully present if you have heart disease? How can you be fully present if you have a broken leg? How can you be fully present if you are sick? Well, if people are sick, we need to get them well. And then we need to keep them well. The concept really got me excited. When you think about it, it isn't as if we're going to turn ourselves into a doctor, but we should be able to raise awareness and provide the resources to our employees and their families so they can focus on what's important."

The quest to create a fully present workforce took off like a rocket. "In our discussions, we asked, are you really fully present if you are worried about your finances?" David said. "The answer is no. Some of our employees in California have a really tough time affording a home. Should we be financial planners and mortgage bankers? No, but we should provide easy access to the people with the skills that can help."

Medtronic has a program called *Total Well Being*, specifically aimed at creating a workforce that is fully present. It helps employees deal with issues like elder care, financial security, and personal health. "We're providing dieticians to counsel people on how to lower blood pressure, and we've developed day care centers and child care access in most of our offices," David explained. Carefully chosen words like *fully present* help propel Medtronic to the top of the list of America's best places to work.

Efficient Language

Sometimes the best lessons can be learned from watching children. The fourth graders who attend Camp St. Croix learn a great lesson. Camp St. Croix is a typical wilderness camp, but during the school season, it hosts field trips for city kids to teach them how to be good stewards of nature. Within minutes of arrival, all of the kids are seated together on the floor to discuss the concept of "waste." Counselors teach how wasting affects nature. Then, in a burst of calculated cleverness, the head counselor proclaims, "At Camp St. Croix, we do not allow *food waste*." Of course, the kids snicker with quizzical smirks. "*Food waste* is a problem because, like all other waste, it requires energy and resources for transportation and disposal. It requires paper and plastic to take it to the garbage, it requires gasoline to haul it away, and it takes up space in a landfill."

Now, you and I both know that food doesn't take up very much space in a landfill. However, the counselors really wanted kids to understand the importance of cleaning their plates. How many times have you had trouble getting a kid to clean a dinner plate? The kids at Camp St. Croix did not want to contribute to the waste in the world, so they easily bought into the concept of "no food waste." Over the period of two-and-a-half days—seven meals—100 kids produced less than 14 ounces of food waste. Now that's efficient use of language.

How can we apply the lessons of Camp St. Croix to our leadership? Look around at some of the highest-performing cultures. You'll start to notice they've developed a language all their own. They have their own versions of "no food waste." The benefit of creating such a language is less fragmentation of effort—people all working towards the same end, with the same expectation.

Creating Uniform Expectations

When building business development programs, I believe it's very important to create a specific vocabulary. We start by eliminating the concept of "selling." Most people in professional services hate to "sell." But they can more easily handle the concepts of "outreach," or "courting perfect clients." Both concepts help to disarm the queasiness around "sales." Then, developing a uniform expectation around specific words helps accelerate acceptance and build permanency. Words like "Discovery," "First Meetings," "Relationship Manager," and "Scouts" all take on a specific meaning, and that creates remarkable efficiency. When pursuing an opportunity, everyone knows what to expect from one another: What questions to ask, what steps to follow, and how to spot a quality engagement.

One specific business development program centers on this intentional concept: "We will build our business by pursuing and attracting *significant clients of choice*." Those words, *significant clients of choice*, have become the mantra for everything that is done in that firm. *Significant* means two things:

1. Companies have the capacity to invest in our services to a sufficient degree to accomplish tangible results; and,

2. The client has meaningful challenges that will help our people learn new skills and grow as professionals.

Clients of Choice Also Means Two Things:

1. The clients are decent people who can be respected and will respect us; and,

2. The company name will reflect positively on the firm when mentioned as a client.

Of course, the leader could have said:

We will build our business by attracting clients who have the capacity to invest enough in our services to accomplish tangible results, and have meaningful challenges that will help our people learn new skills and grow as professionals, and are decent people who can be respected, and will respect us, and, the company name will reflect positively on the firm when mentioned as a client.

Whew! *Significant clients of choice* works better. It's simple, straightforward, and memorable.

Using Simple Word Labels

Many other examples of naming things are available to draw upon. One of my favorites is from the people at Pfizer, Inc., who literally created the "sexual health" industry by introducing Viagra® and using the term *erectile dysfunction (ED)* instead of impotence. Before the term erectile dysfunction became a household word, people—men in particular—shied away from the word *impotence*, and all of the baggage that came with "being impotent." The intentional use of the language *erectile dysfunction* gave men and women everywhere—including the media—permission to talk about something that previously was taboo. Admittedly, the success of Viagra is yet another example of Western capitalism in its finest hour. However, the real power can be felt by couples, patients, and physicians all over the globe, who now have much easier language to use when addressing a super-sensitive subject.

Another example comes from the automobile industry. The rush towards leasing new cars in the late 80s and 90s created a glut of late-model used cars. With inventories of used cars rising, many dealers were forced to become more intentional about dealing with the concerns of potential buyers. Some buyers thought a used vehicle might be a bargain upfront, but a money pit down the road. Still others thought, *Why should I buy a hard-driven lemon when I can "rent" a brand new car for less per month?*

To alleviate the concerns of both types of buyers, dealers invested heavily in demonstrating the fitness of their used cars. Some simply touted the virtues of their service staff, bragging about the years of talent represented by their mechanics. But a few were very intentional about creating a "101-Point Checklist" to certify the condition of the vehicle.

The 101-Point Checklist provides a document—a lesson learned in *Commandment #7: Put It on Paper*—but the difference is more significant. In the first scenario, the dealer is asking the buyer to "trust" that his mechanics have thoroughly inspected the car and everything is in good working condition. How much does anyone *really* trust someone associated with a car dealership? The 101-Point Checklist is more vivid, and provides a framework by which the buyer can place his or her trust. The mechanics in the first scenario might actually review 202 items. But the fact of the matter is this—the 101-Point Checklist is more powerful than "trust me"—especially from a car dealer. If you have a highly volatile, low-trust situation that requires your leadership, develop your own 101-Point Checklist to help you gain trust.

Vision Building Made Simple

My favorite business book is called *Built to Last: The Successful Habits of Visionary Companies*, written by James C. Collins and Jerry I. Porras. The book is special for many reasons, one of which is the introduction of the term "Big Hairy Audacious Goal." "BHAG" (pronounced bee-hag) has quickly spread as a vision-building concept. In the confusion of mission and vision, BHAG simplifies the rhetoric and focuses all of the communication energy on one simple thing: The wildest dream of the collective organization. Suddenly, companies were writing Big Hairy Audacious Goals that really resonated with people, injecting personality and emotion into "the mission statement." I've helped numerous organizations to develop their own BHAGs. The process is much more invigorating than "writing a mission statement," and it tends to help leaders avoid taking themselves too seriously. If you haven't read *Built to Last*, you should.

Lynn Casey, whom we met in Commandment #6, intentionally uses the term "personal contracts" when helping people work together. The result is that people shoot straight about what they expect from each other, regardless of rank in the organization. When people create a "personal contract," each party is given permission to hold the other accountable. When senior talent demands specific things from junior talent, the junior has the right to ask for specific things in return. The concept of the personal contract helps keep working relationships connected, especially in the professional services industry where client needs always take a priority over personal needs.

Clearing Up Confusion

Over the years, I've encountered many situations where leaders unintentionally created misunderstanding by using poor word labels. Once, a leader called a big meeting to discuss the virtues of "Project 125." As the only outside consultant, I was secretly hoping the purpose or function of Project 125 would magically reveal itself. But only two of the other ten people in the room were showing they were in sync. Finally, curiosity won out over decorum. *"What the heck is Project 125? Am I the only one who doesn't get it?"* I asked. Of course, Project 125 meant nothing to most of us. In a side conversation, we renamed Project 125 to "Project More 4 Less." From that day on, people understood that the organization was trying to be better coordinated in an effort to get more impact from their communication with less time, energy, and money wasted.

Another client had created an indifferent, almost cynical climate towards the leadership team because of a poorly labeled newsletter. Company information about profitability, operations, and milestones were seldom shared in their culture. The information that was shared with the employee population was circulated via a newsletter called *Management News*. This company has several divisions, with labor unions active in many of those divisions. The name *Management News* was by its very nature adversarial with the union laborers. By simply redesigning the cover and changing the name to *Companywide Update*, the publication and the information it contained received much higher acceptance.

Altered Meanings

One of the common labels that creates tension is the use of the word *committee*. The word *"committee"* universally means "lots of meetings," which sometimes also can translate to "where nothing gets done." By their very nature, committees are chronic—meaning the commitment is regular and never seems to go away. Some people all-out refuse to serve on committees because they prefer getting things done, instead of *talking about* getting things done.

With the pace of our world today, volunteers—whether in the charitable, or in the corporate setting—are getting harder and harder to recruit. Choosing the word *task force* seems to help. "Task force" triggers a different attitude—it suggests there is a beginning and an end, with a specific accomplishment in mind. It's also possible for people to serve effectively on a task force and never attend a single meeting. It's hard to imagine the same for a committee.

Often I hear people in business create unnecessary tension by misusing a political term. The word *issue* almost always puts individuals on the defensive. *Issues* are emotionally loaded concepts—problems—that involve lots of people and intense debate. However, most of the time when people use the word *issue* they really mean "something I want to discuss," or an "action item."

Choosing the right words can also help leaders deal with performance issues on their teams. Many leaders, especially feelers and talkers, invest themselves heavily in getting to know the people important to their success. And sometimes they let personal attachment get in the way of honest performance evaluation. Workplace psychologists recommend that leaders use these words: *The job isn't getting done.* Those carefully chosen words can help frame a performance issue and diffuse the emotional conflict that can spiral out of control.

Commandment #8
Practical Tactical Tips

Try these practical tactical tips to help you apply *Commandment #8: Be Careful What You Call Things,* to your leadership:

Develop a "phrase that pays."

Significant clients of choice is an excellent example of a phrase that pays—an *intentional set of language* that is memorable, meaningful, and easy to repeat. Identify the key points of your leadership and craft the words you want repeated.

Read your organization's marketing materials and literature.

How long has it been since you did that? Take them home and read them. Circle word labels and concepts that work really well, and also the ones that are confusing or misleading. Share this list with your staff and ask them to *be careful what they call things*.

Look carefully at the people who report to you, and identify where "the job isn't getting done."

Enabling poor performers slowly decays the morale of the people who really are getting the job done. Perhaps the poor performers don't understand they aren't measuring up; if that's the case, it really is your problem. Schedule a "the job isn't getting done" discussion with them.

Commandment #9: Let Your Enthusiasm Light the Fire

> Nothing significant was ever accomplished without enthusiasm.
> —Ralph Waldo Emerson

BILL GATES, THE WEALTHIEST PERSON ON THE PLANET, IS A BRILLIANT MAN—a wizard in many respects. But when asked about the driving force behind his success, he replied: "What I do best is share my enthusiasm." The lesson here is simple: If you aren't excited about what's important to you, then you can't expect anyone else to be excited either. On my desk is a neatly framed quotation from B.C. Forbes, founder of *Forbes* magazine:

> *Search and you will find that at the base and birth of every great organization was an enthusiast, someone consumed with earnestness of purpose, with confidence in their powers, with faith in the worthwhileness of their endeavors.*

Forbes reminds me to focus on the joy of my profession, to emphasize the positive energy in my day-to-day work. What are you excited about? If you're having trouble building consensus or motivating people to change, ask yourself: *Am I excited about this?* If you're not, reengineer the situation, starting with yourself. Because *your* enthusiasm lights the fire. Ralph Waldo Emerson's insight rings like the chimes at midnight: *Nothing significant was ever accomplished without enthusiasm.*

Consistent enthusiasm creates magnetism that pulls people together. Negativity pushes them apart. We've all heard the sociological truism: People will share a positive experience (attitude) with two people, and a negative experience (attitude) with ten. Whether this is true or not, we all understand the power of enthusiasm for the negative. If positive enthusiasm is the pilot light that keeps the furnace alive, enthusiasm for the negative will start a forest fire that will burn your house down.

Why is that so? Because negativity permeates so much of our society today. People are cynical, shaped by marketers and politicians making false promises. It doesn't take a genius to see that we are being bombarded with negative messages. Graphic news stories grab the headlines and open the evening news. Country music titles: *Take This Job and Shove It, I Ain't Working Here No More.* Rap titles too graphic for me to want to print. Negativity sells.

But you can't go there. If your leadership is respected, your voice rings louder than you realize. People are watching and listening. The second you slip into the negative, you've started a cancer.

People Listen for Enthusiasm

When powerful leaders say things with enthusiasm, people listen. A client was famous for saying: "You know, what really keeps me up at night is *[fill in the blank]*." A simple statement. However, she said it so often a negative pattern was emerging, and people were starting to be concerned. Her trusted colleagues wondered when the last time was that she had said anything positive. "I'm just being a realist," she offered defensively when being coached.

Gradually she realized a simple truth—how could she expect people to be engaged and excited if they didn't think she, *herself,* was engaged and excited? Soon she began to mix in a few "You-know-what-gets-me-excited-about-this-business" comments with the "You-know-what-really-keeps-me-up-at-night" phrases. The people around her noticed.

When was the last time you told people what you're excited about? Have you thought about what gets you out of bed in the morning before the alarm? The people important to your success need to hear it over and over again. It's your job to counteract the negative.

Of course, you can't be fake or promote false hope. People expect you to be real. But you can't cross that fine line between sharing real concerns and being enthusiastic for the negative.

Learning the Hard Way

A few years ago, in the public relations business, we were engaged in a terrific project. That particular year, it consumed more than a quarter of our people. They were busy, happy, productive, and very profitable. At the busiest moment, I needed help courting a new client. In a moment of insanity, I blurted out this stupid comment: *"I can't wait till this damn project is finally done. We've got other fish to fry or we won't eat tomorrow."* And I said it with enthusiasm! Of course, several young staffers heard me, and the words cut deep. Luckily a partner had the courage to pull me aside and point out the effect it had on his team. I still think about that mistake today. It took lots of effort to rebuild a positive balance in my savings bank of goodwill with those people.

It All Starts With You

Tom Lee is a picture of enthusiasm. He's the principal of Normandale Hills Elementary School in Bloomington, Minnesota. What a tough job. I watched my mom serve as an elementary school music teacher for 25 years. Sure, she had her summers off, but I can't think of a tougher job than being a teacher or principal.

"Teaching children isn't as easy as it used to be—at least not here," Tom explained. Bloomington is an upper-middle-class suburb of Minneapolis-St. Paul. "Our student mix has changed dramatically. In four years, we've gone from totally lily-white complexions, to a mix of worldly colors. And today, we have 14 different languages that are spoken in the home. Many times the child has to serve as the interpreter between the school and the parent." But despite the changing face of Normandale Hills Elementary, the school itself remains a harbor of positive energy. Tom starts every school day with a rousing imitation of Robin Williams in the movie *Good Morning, Vietnam.* "Goooooood Mor Ning, Nor Man Dale Hiiiiiiilllllllllzzzz!" he sings through the intercom system. That enthusiasm carries the day.

"If I'm not excited about learning, how can I expect my staff to be excited about learning and teaching? And if the kids aren't excited about school, how can we expect the parents to be excited about school?" he said. "The things we're teaching today are terrific. We have computers and field trips and wonderful teachers who are shaping the leaders of tomorrow."

But with the ever-widening gap of family backgrounds, it's not always easy to stay on top. "I go out of my way to keep things simple around here," he continued. "The only question that really counts is 'What's best for the kids?' Of course, we can disagree about what's best for the kids, but we don't ever let a kid issue get overshadowed by an adult issue. It's the adult issues that tend to take the wind out of our sails . . . our enthusiasm swells when we talk about kids. So we keep the focus on the kids."

Tom's enthusiasm for his job came from his childhood. "When I was a kid, I watched many, many people in my Michigan home town go off to jobs they hated. I was determined not to let that happen to me," he said. "That experience sticks with me every day. I want my staff to love their jobs—because if they love teaching, the kids will love learning.

"It sounds so simple, but just the other day I was reminded again about how important that is. I had a conversation with a dentist I met at a hockey game. I admitted that I really hate going to the dentist . . . the smell, the sound of the drill. I just get cold and clammy, and I want to get out of there as fast as I can. But the dentist turned back to me and said, 'That's how I feel when I enter a school. The smells, the sounds, just throw me back to a time that wasn't fun. I hated elementary school.' If that isn't motivation to make a difference, I don't know what is! Chances are that dentist's children are going to hate school, unless someone like me does something to make a difference."

Of course, Tom's brand of enthusiasm might not be appropriate for your setting. When I've seen him in all-school parent meetings, his enthusiasm can be a little overkill with some parents. But when you look at their kids, they are energized by his enthusiasm. Most Normandale Hills kids would rather be at school than anywhere else. His enthusiasm lights their fire, and that's terrific leadership.

You've Got To Sell It

I recently read about the late Father William Cunningham, co-founder of Focus: HOPE. He and Eleanor Josaitis founded a world-class organization for young people after the 1967 riots in Detroit. Deep in the mires of urban blight, they helped thousands of young people learn machinist and life skills as a means to breaking out of the cycle. In an annual stakeholders meeting he said something that underscores the need for enthusiasm in leadership. "As leaders, we don't set the goals high enough for our people. Leadership is salesmanship. Getting people to say, 'C'mon, we can do this!'"

The power of his statement is the passion. Pam Shaw Hargrove, the detail-oriented finance expert we met in Commandment #3, shares Father Cunningham's perspective. "I think it's really important to let people know you believe in what you are doing," she said. "And sometimes that means you just have to sell it! There was a particular moment in my corporate days when our financial situation was rather bleak. The management had been deceived by a person who really didn't have a handle on the bottom line. [In] my first big meeting, I had to share the bad news. But I found some things to be optimistic about. Then I looked them in the eye and convinced them we finally had the real numbers, and that I thought we could work our way out. I was brand new, and I needed to convince them I knew what I was doing. Sometimes you just have to sell it, and sell it hard to gain the respect you deserve."

Again, if you aren't excited about what's important to you, then how can you expect anyone else to be excited either? The Reverend Jerry Hoffman is a retired pastor, and the chairman of the board of directors of Lutheran Social Service of Minnesota. In his own words, Jerry is firmly engaged in "re-firement," not retirement. From his energy, you get the feeling he could run a Fortune 500 company. What he's brought to the board is enthusiasm for governance. Governance? Yes, the policies and procedures by which the board goes about its work. Until I met Jerry, the practice of governance for me was like a trip to the dentist for Tom Lee. But by his sheer enthusiasm, the board is engaged in implementing the Carver system—a Policy Governance model that is changing the way public and non-profit boards are operating all over the world.

It wasn't easy. The LSS board first read and discussed a book, then listened to a guest speaker, and eventually got help from a consultant. Most people were still dazed and unsure about the reasons to make the change. The common wisdom, "If it ain't broke, don't fix it," was fully in force. But Jerry was unwavering in his mission. He's a student of high-functioning boards and has witnessed organizations that have faded because they didn't seek out, or embrace, better governance. "I've seen governance work in very powerful ways," he explained. "My last congregation used this model. It got us out of discussing the nagging little things in the church, and turned our vision towards the future."

His credibility and enthusiasm for policy governance magnetically pulled the LSS board together. Even though many still didn't see the magic, we believed it could be true. If our chair could get that fired up about "policy governance," then we should give him the benefit of the doubt and move forward.

Energizing Everyone, Every Time

The root of sharing enthusiasm comes from the belief that your work really matters. Noel M. Tichy and Eli Cohen wrote in *The Leadership Engine:* "Powerful leaders pay attention to creating positive energy the same way they pay attention to spreading ideas and teaching values. That's because they know that positive energy helps people overcome obstacles and rise to new challenges." Carlos Cantu, retired CEO of ServiceMaster, backs that up, and sets a really high standard for himself. "At the end of the day, I feel, every single person has got to come away from a meeting with me with something positive. My goal is that at every single session, people feel they've gained something from the experience."

Go back to your Humble Sandwich. What did you write down for "The three things people like about me?" Do people feel energized by you? If not, you have the potential to really grow. Whether you realize it or not, the people important to your success really want to know what excites you. Especially when times are tough, business is down, and the obstacles are mounting, you can be the catalyst to get the fires burning again. Let your enthusiasm light the fire.

Commandment #9
Practical Tactical Tips

Try these practical tactical tips to help you apply *Commandment #9: Let Your Enthusiasm Light the Fire,* to your leadership:

Write down what excites you about your current situation.

Keep it within sight. Start your meetings by sharing this information. You will be more interesting and more persuasive.

Start asking people: What are you working on that is exciting?

Listen carefully, and respond by sharing what excites you.

Spend time with people who are enthusiastic about their lives.

Enthusiasm is contagious. Start paying attention to others and avoid people who demonstrate enthusiasm for the negative.

Commandment #10: Don't Get Defensive

> Organizations don't make decisions, only individuals create a climate of fear and control.
> —Harvard Business Review

LEADERS HAVE ALWAYS BEEN SUBJECT TO MORE CRITICISM THAN THEY DESERVE. Challenges to your leadership are healthy. We should all wish for a talented team of people who think with their own minds and challenge our thinking. Challenges keep us sharp, attentive, and fit to handle our jobs. But when those challenges begin to cut more deeply than your comfort level, you need to be prepared to handle them. Developing a sensible, sensitive way to avoid being defensive is the ultimate test of your character. Because when you get defensive, all of the excellent rapport you've developed by following the first nine commandments can vanish in an instant.

Think back on your career. There are moments you wish you could live over. It's amazing how the smallest of incidents can escalate into a catfight. It's not uncommon to see people walk away from meetings steaming and stewing, silently vowing to wage a counterattack. Defensive emotions are very powerful, capable of turning even the smallest, meekest house cat into a scary, shrieking monster. When our inner self is threatened, we can do things beyond our imaginations. However, when you deal with an aggressive challenge to your leadership in a cool, calm, dignified manner, you can make significant deposits into your personal savings bank of goodwill.

Here is a simple strategy to help you keep your emotions in check. It comes from the principles of crisis management. When you recognize a challenging encounter, you can fall back on this three-step procedure to avoid being defensive:

Step 1: First, show concern.

Step 2: Listen for understanding.

Step 3: Ask for help in resolving the issue.

Cooler Heads Prevail

Within months of joining the board of directors at Lutheran Social Service, I found myself at the center of a very controversial situation. For 50 years, LSS has been the steward of the pristine peninsula between Turtle Lake and Lower White Fish Lake in Minnesota, one of the most beautiful pieces of property in all of the northland. On the crest of the hill sits Camp Knutson—a special-needs camp for children and their families who live every day with cancer, skin disease, autism, and other illnesses. Each summer, more than 200 children experience the great outdoors with the help of LSS staff, special health-care workers, and the care and attention from people all over the county.

A crisis was in the making because Camp Knutson

was losing money. And, worse yet, the facilities were
badly in need of repair. At a board meeting, this question
was raised:

> *With nearly a mile of shoreline, on one of the
> most beautiful sites in all of Minnesota, are we
> being the best stewards of this property by losing
> money, and serving only a very small number of
> children? With property values escalating rapidly,
> we may be able to transfer the land to a devel-
> oper, build a world-class camp on another site,
> and have enough money left over for an endow-
> ment to ensure its future.*

As word of this discussion spread through the community, people were outraged. Over a period of 50 years,
families had invested themselves deeply in the mission of
the camp by making quilts for the beds, planting flowers,
and caring for ailing buildings. Most thought of Camp
Knutson as "their camp," and rightfully so. The emotions quickly escalated into letters to the editors of local
and regional newspapers, with sharply worded criticism
aimed at LSS executives and board members. The attacks
were personal and they cut deep.

As a member of the Camp Knutson Task Force, I felt
we had no choice but to meet the challenges head on. We
sat through dozens of personal meetings with angry
people. I personally answered every one of the 43 letters I
received—some of them targeting me directly with harsh
criticism.

Here's how the three-step process worked to help us
avoid being defensive:

First, Show Concern.

Without raising my voice in the personal meetings, I agreed with their concern—to abandon the peninsula and destroy Camp Knutson would be terrible, and definitely unfair to all of the people who have invested so much of their lives in the camp.

Second, Listen for Understanding.

I heard people express their frustration over "having no control" over this terrible situation. Everyone had a different reason for being angry, but they all had one thing in common—writing letters and protesting seemed to be their only course of action to "fight back." By listening, I was able to get to a point where they would actually listen to me (some needed more "listening to" than others).

Third, Ask for Help in Resolving the Issue

The "issue" was really a financial crisis. The board did not intend to destroy, eliminate, or abandon Camp Knutson. It was quite the opposite. Our goal was to preserve the camp, and ensure its future for generations to come. When the angry individuals were ready to listen, I restated the issue—using their words—and asked for help. My part of the conversation went like this.

We are deeply committed to the mission of the camp. And although the land and facilities were donated to LSS years ago, there hasn't been adequate funding to keep the camp up to date. What most people don't know is that we are continually operating at a substantial loss, and there needs to *be an investment of nearly $3 million just to bring the camp up to code. And then the camp needs another $2 million to secure its future for generations to come. We're open to solutions; we'd rather not sell the property.*

Soon the controversy turned into community triumph. Camp Knutson supporters united in their frustration, and delivered an alternative solution. Today, LSS and the community are jointly engaged in a capital campaign to raise the money and keep the camp where it belongs.

However, the situation could have turned out much differently. Those strong emotions manifested themselves in some very nasty letters. And it doesn't take too many letters challenging your motives, your morals, and your integrity to make a person a little defensive! The task force showed remarkable courage, and cooler heads prevailed.

Angry Customers— An Opportunity to Improve

This same process can be applied to your interaction with angry, dissatisfied customers. Following is a letter written to a client of a professional services firm. It serves as an example of how to approach a tricky situation without being defensive:

Dear [name of client]:

As my colleague and I prepare to visit you early next month, I feel compelled to be clear about our intentions. We are on a mission of understand-

ing—trying to make right what went wrong. Of course, the prospect of working together in the future looks dim. Nonetheless, our firm is built on a fundamental principle of client satisfaction, and we take it seriously. You and your colleagues certainly know that reputation is everything in the service business. If you'll be straightforward with us, we'll promise to listen and do the same with you. In examining our relationship, we know that it's not that uncommon for misunderstandings to arise shortly after "the honeymoon period." Both our firms were moving awfully fast, without much time for the necessary education on either end. In my opinion, one very critical step was skipped upfront. We have recently implemented a special meeting as part of our client satisfaction methodology, designed specifically to help avoid what happened to our two firms. We'd like to use the same set of discussion points when we meet. My assistant will work out the exact time and date for the meeting. Thanks in advance for the opportunity to meet again.

A dissatisfied client is two things: A challenge to avoid being defensive, and an opportunity to improve. The letter referenced above was taken from an actual incident. The meeting actually happened. The client was willing to share the blame for the dissatisfaction, and today the two firms are still working together.

Success Depends on Understanding

Adrienne Diercks, founder of Project Success, often deals with people challenging the value of her enterprise. She has developed a remarkable applied-learning model for helping troubled and disadvantaged adolescents build life aspirations by experiencing live theater. The students immerse themselves in the plot, study the characters, and discuss how it relates to their current lives. Through facilitation, the students learn how to set goals for a better life in the future.

Her most memorable, significant challenge happened early in the development of the program. Adrienne recalled: "I was hosting a meeting with the teaching staff at one of my first schools when a powerful teacher stood and shouted: *'I don't like this. I don't believe it's going to make a difference. I think it's a waste of time, and I don't want the distraction with my children, in my classroom.'* I was stunned. Here I was, trying to win the support of the teaching staff, and I'd been publicly attacked. All I could do was say: *'I'm sorry. You don't have to participate. I don't ever want you to do something like this if you think it's wrong for your kids.'* The teacher said, *'Good,'* and marched away.

"I never forgot about that. During the school year, many of the kids in that teacher's class would come up to me and ask, *'Why can't we go to the plays, too?'* I could have said: *'Go ask your teacher,'* but I didn't. I just made sure the kids received tickets so they could go anyway. And later in the year, I circled back to that teacher." Adrienne didn't want to cause a scene, but she realized that she needed to know what caused such a strong reaction from this teacher, because it was likely someone else might feel the same way.

"We had a wonderful meeting. I learned some things about Project Success that affected people in ways that I couldn't see," she said. "I spent a lot of time that summer fixing the problems, and my first meeting in the fall was with that teacher. I showed the changes that 'we had made together,' and the teacher signed on. We're still working together today and that teacher is one of our strongest supporters—the one who stands up at the teachers' meetings saying: '*Whatever we do, we have to keep doing Project Success.*'"

That brings a smile to Adrienne's face. Things could have been different. They could have gone sour quickly if Adrienne had lost her head in that first meeting and fired back defensively. But she didn't. Her mission was to benefit every single kid in that school. Without the support of every teacher, the kids would be the ones who would lose out, not Adrienne herself. She acknowledged the concern, listened carefully for understanding, and asked for help in creating a mutually rewarding solution.

Managing Up, Down and All Around

Mark Peterson, the CEO of Lutheran Social Service of Minnesota (LSS), whom we met in Commandment #5, deals regularly with people of all creeds and colors, and all economic conditions. Mark has a complicated job and on top of it all, as we learned in Commandment #9, the current chair of the board, the Reverend Hoffman, is suggesting a dramatic change to how the organization is governed. The fundamental principle is a set of clearly articulated "boundaries," which are presented in negative language that the CEO must stay within.

As most CEOs understand, a good working relationship with the board is critical to success. Mark has achieved a great deal of success, aided by a very good working relationship with his board. Anyone in his shoes could easily apply the "if it ain't broke, don't fix it" philosophy, and feel a bit defensive about the suggestion that things need to be changed.

The first board discussions were clumsy and mildly tense until Mark showed that he wasn't going to be defensive. He offered this commentary during the deliberations: "I realize this process could have a profound effect on the role of the CEO. I think this is a pretty darn good job . . . I operate with a great deal of autonomy today. But don't worry about me. I'm troubled by some of the language, and I'm not sure how I'll deal with some of the boundaries, but I think this is a good thing. I hear the excitement in your voices when we talk about the future. And if this new governance model is going to keep the board engaged and help keep us focused on achieving a prosperous future, then I'm all for it. Even if I don't fully understand it yet!"

The rewards of *don't get defensive* are obvious. People will notice. They will treat you with respect, and come to you freely with criticism and praise. That's what excellent leaders want.

Commandment #10
Practical Tactical Tips

Try these practical tactical tips to help you apply *Commandment #10: Don't Get Defensive* to your leadership:

Start to notice when people around you get defensive.

Write down the process and post it in a place you can see it: *First, show concern, listen for understanding, and ask for help.* Study how you would respond differently than the people you are observing.

Coach your people on how to use the three-step approach in their work.

It will help you apply it to yourself.

Catch yourself.

Ask your most trusted colleague to help you identify the signs of when you are getting defensive. Does your neck start to get red? Do you cross your arms and fidget? Do you look away and shut down? Learn the signals, and catch yourself. Then start to apply the model to yourself: *First, show concern, listen for understanding, and ask for help.* Once you've caught yourself starting to feel defensive, it becomes easier to identify and tackle.

Chapter 11:
Repeat, Repeat,
Repeat

> Consistency disarms the cynic.
> —Unknown

IN BUSINESS, "CHAPTER 11" MEANS BANKRUPTCY. It's not too far a stretch to make the same connection to leadership. Repetition is under-appreciated. Without consistently repeating your most important messages, your effectiveness erodes and your savings bank of goodwill can go bankrupt.

Repeat, repeat, repeat. Your consistency demonstrates your convictions—not only consistent words but also consistent actions. Recently, a CEO coaching client shared his frustrations about the news from a company-wide employee confidence survey. "The most difficult news to hear when you are the CEO is that not everyone on your senior team is walking the talk," he said. "It's not enough for us to talk about what's important—people all around us are watching to see if we are all in sync . . . telling the same story, asking the same questions, and most importantly, demonstrating the same leadership behaviors. It is tough work because the resisting forces—the cynics—feast on inconsistencies."

The Enemy Within

Over the years, I've noticed that achievement-oriented people have one thing in common—their minds work really fast. Men, women, CEOs, managers, farmers, and entrepreneurs alike—it seems to have nothing to do with education or job orientation. The achievers process a lot of information from multiple sources quickly. It's an obvious advantage but also a curse. The enemy they face is their own boredom: Many of the most powerful ideas are conceived well before the first time they are communicated. Leaders have bounced the idea around in their brains for days, weeks, or months until they are comfortable with the concept. I like to call this "intellectual ping pong." By the time the idea has been swatted back and forth across the filters in the brain, it has become familiar. Comfortable. Old information. Once the energy has been expended to communicate the concept with others, it's tempting to move on to the next thing. But this would be a mistake. Repetition is crucial to keeping the concept alive.

Madison Avenue Magic

Whether it's true or not, the advertising rule of thumb applies: people need to hear or see a message seven times before they remember it—and 77 times before they'll actually do anything about it! Your personal experience probably validates this claim. How many emails and voicemails did you get today? How many memos, postcards, letters, or advertising circulars were in your mailbox? Like it or not, you are engaged in a sophisticated battle for the attention of the people important to your success. The challenge is to cut through the noise so you can be heard. Not only heard, but understood! One of your best strategies is to repeat, repeat, repeat.

It often helps to think of your leadership as a campaign, such as the Madison Avenue advertising campaigns for powerful consumer products. Recently I collided with an exceptionally well-developed campaign for minivans. In preparation for a cross-country family driving vacation, I visited the Dodge dealership for a tune-up. As I entered the service doors, a red and white sign introduced me to the concept of "Stow 'n Go." It's a new system where the seats in the back of the minivan can be folded *into the floor* when you need the space for cargo. The basic benefit is not having to lift those heavy seats out. In the lobby, posters reminded me that this company was the first to introduce the minivan concept, the first to introduce the concept of putting *wheels* on the bottom of minivan seats for easy removal, and now the first to create the Stow 'n Go option. The message was "we are the innovators, and we've done it again." You've seen campaigns like this. If it would have stopped there, I probably would have forgotten. But it didn't.

In the lobby, I watched a DVD being played on a flat-screen TV showing computer animation of the seats effortlessly folding into the floor. It caused me to vividly recall the first time I removed the back bench seat from our first minivan. I had no idea the seats were so heavy. Without the proper lifting technique, I wrenched my back. The concept of Stow 'n Go was getting more appealing. As I left the dealer, I was given a handsome leather keychain and a glossy service receipt folder prominently featuring—you guessed it—the Stow 'n Go seating system.

Three days later, we received a customer service questionnaire in the mail. What did the envelope say? Stow 'n Go, of course. The next day, our family email address received a Stow 'n Go animated email begging to be double-clicked. And to top it off, the lead television commercial before *ER* that week was none other than Stow 'n Go. We collided many more times with this campaign—and we've actually talked about how nice the Stow 'n Go concept would be if we hadn't just bought a new van 13 months ago!

Building Your Campaign

Is this simply good marketing? Yes. Is it overkill? Maybe so. But the point isn't hard to translate to leadership. Your leadership themes have a better chance of sticking if they are merchandised like Stow 'n Go. The wisdom is in the simplicity and the repetition. If you can boil your aspirations down to the content of a matchbook cover or a "bumper sticker," you are well on your way to a campaign that will boost your effectiveness.

Basically, you are applying *Leadership Communication Commandment #8: Be Careful What You Call Things* in a practical way that allows you—and others around you—to repeat the message in meaningful ways. Here are examples of some of the "bumper stickers" that I know are in use by excellent leaders today:

- Precise Placement
- Wow Photography

- A Movement of Hope
- Clients for Life
- The Best at Next
- Getting to Green
- Performance Culture

Without context, they don't mean much. It's the leader's passion, energy, and consistent interpretation that make the bumper stickers come to life. It's not simply the job of the communications department to package these concepts or advance them as ideas. It's a function of leadership to deliberately shape the hearts and minds of people by continually reminding them about what's most important.

Accepting the campaign mentality helps you pull together the leadership communication concepts you read about in this book and put them to work:

- Be visual—develop a graphic, a model, or a set of word pictures that will make your bumper sticker visual. Repeat the use of these visuals over and over again.

- Tell stories—develop your own set of "signature stories" that bring your most important leadership concepts to life. Repeat your success stories in every staff meeting, every company-wide speech, and every committee meeting.

- Put it in writing—capture your thinking and the important conversations about your leadership concepts in recap memos, philosophy statements, and letters to customers.

- Practice "no surprises"—you are successful when people are surprised that you *didn't* talk about your bumper sticker.

Remember, we are our own worst enemy. We get bored too quickly with powerful concepts that others are just getting accustomed to. And we become far too familiar—even desensitized—to concepts we've thought about for a long time. They might be crystal clear to you, but you probably haven't shared them often enough to make the concepts mean the same thing up and down the hall or across the company.

Beyond the perils of boredom and familiarity, there will be other reasons to think you should change your message. A small number of people will always roll their eyes, telling you with their body language *"here it comes again, I've heard this a thousand times before."* And yet, the masses will give you their hearts and minds because you are building confidence through consistency.

Want proof? Ask individual team members or employees what they remembered most about the last important team meeting you led. Listen carefully. Do they have the answers on the tip of their tongue, or do they struggle to recall what the meeting was even about? If you are lucky, they will be able to articulate three or four things they remember. Let's hope it's what you wanted them to remember. If not, it's time to repeat, repeat, repeat. Because *if people don't understand you, it's your problem, not theirs.*

Chapter 11
Practical Tactical Tips

Try these practical tactical tips to help you apply *Repeat, Repeat, Repeat* to your leadership:

Do a real-time reality check.

Perform your own survey by asking people what they think is most important to the business. Listen carefully and take notes. Share what you heard in your next team meeting. How does it match with what you think is important?

Build a bumper sticker.

Boil down your strategic plan into the fewest words possible. You don't need the gift of a Madison Avenue copywriter. Just try it. Bounce your concepts off a colleague. Force yourself to reduce the message to the amount of information that could be put on a matchbook, a tee-shirt, or a bumper sticker.

Audit yourself for inconsistencies.

Review your own correspondence—emails, memos, meeting agendas. Ask your colleagues and team members for specific examples of where your words and behaviors (and *their* words and behaviors) are both consistent and inconsistent.

Develop signature stories that you can repeat.

Ask your colleagues for anecdotes and stories—

either from you or from around the organization—that best illustrate the struggles and triumphs people are feeling with the strategic direction of your organization. Repeat them in meetings, speeches, and email correspondence to help keep people aligned for success.

Bibliography

Books

Alessandra, Tony J., and Michael J. O'Connor. *The Platinum Rule: Discover the Four Basic Business Personalities—and How They Can Lead You to Success*. New York: Warner Books, Incorporated, 1996.

Buckingham, Marcus, and Curt Coffman. *First, Break All the Rules: What the World's Greatest Managers Do Differently*. New York: Simon and Schuster Trade, May 1999.

Carver, John. *Boards That Make A Difference*. New York: Jossey-Bass, 1997.

Chapman, Gary. *The Five Love Languages: How to Express Heartfelt Commitment to Your Mate*. Chicago: Northfield Publishing, 1995.

Collins, James C., and Jerry I. Porras. *Built to Last: Successful Habits of Visionary Companies*. New York: HarperBusiness, 1994.

Davis, Sandra, and Bill Handschin. *Reinventing Yourself: Life Planning After 50 Using the Strong and the MBTI®*. Palo Alto, CA: Consulting Psychologists Press, Inc., 1998.

Gardner, Howard, and Emma Laskins. *Leading Minds: An Anatomy of Leadership*. Basic Books, May 1996.

Judy, Richard W., and Carol D'Amico. *Workforce 2020: Work and Workers in the 21st Century.* Hudson Institute, March 1997.

Keirsey, David W., and Marilyn Bates. *Please Understand Me: Character and Temperament Types.* Del Mar, CA: Prometheus Nemesis Book Company, May 1985.

Strunk, William, and E. B. White. *Elements of Style.* New York: MacMillian Publishing Company, Inc., July 1999.

Tichy, Noel M. and Eli Cohen. *The Leadership Engine: How Winning Companies Build Leaders at Every Level.* HarperCollins Publishers, Inc., October 1997.

Weiss, Alan. *Million Dollar Consulting: The Professional's Guide to Growing a Practice.* The McGraw-Hill Companies, October 1997.

Articles

Charan, Ram, and Geoffrey Colbin. "Why CEOs Fail." *Fortune,* June 21, 1999.

Conger. Jay A. "The Necessary Art of Persuasion." *Harvard Business Review,* May-June 1998.

Shaw, Gordon, Robert Brown, and Philip Bromiley. "Strategic Stories: How 3M Is Rewriting Business Planning." *Harvard Business Review,* May-June 1998.

Kucharski, Matt. *PR Tactics,* 2000.

Walker Information. "1999 National Employee Benchmark Report." Indianapolis, Indiana: Walker Information, 1999. (www.walkerinfo.com.)

Additional Recommended Readings

Beckwith, Harry. *Selling the Invisible: A Field Guide to Modern Marketing*. New York: Warner Books, Inc., March 1997.

—*The Invisible Touch: The Four Keys to Modern Marketing*. New York: Warner Books, Inc., March 2000.

Carnegie, Dale. *How to Win Friends and Influence People*. New York: Simon and Schuster, June 1982.

—*The Leader in You: How to Win Friends, Influence People and Succeed in a Changing World*. New York: Simon and Schuster, March 1995.

Davenport, Thomas H., and John C. Beck. *The Attention Economy: Understanding the New Currency of Business*. Harvard Business School Press, June 2001.

Dupree, Max. *Leadership Jazz: The Art of Conducting Business through Leadership, Followership, Teamwork, Voice, Touch*. New York: Dell Publishing Company, Inc., September 1993.

Jones, Laurie Beth. *Jesus CEO, Using Ancient Wisdom for Visionary Leadership*. Hyperion, January 1995.

McNally, David. *Even Eagles Need a Push: Learning to Soar in a Changing World*. New York: Dell Publishing Company, Inc., 1994.

Miller, James B., and Paul B. Brown. *The Corporate Coach: How to Build a Team of Loyal Customers and Happy Employees*. New York: Harper Business, March 1994.

Scott, Steven K. *Simple Steps to Impossible Dreams: The 15 Power Secrets of the World's Most Successful People.* New York: Simon and Schuster, 1998.

Shapiro, Ronald M., and Mark A. Jankowski. *The Power of Nice: How to Negotiate So Everyone Wins— Especially You!* New York: John Wiley and Sons, Inc., 1998.

Worksheets

The Humble Sandwich®

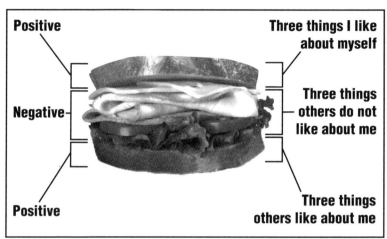

Positive		Three things I like about myself
Negative		Three things others do not like about me
Positive		Three things others like about me

Three things I like about myself:

1. _____

2. _____

3. _____

The three things I know others don't like about me:

1. _____

2. _____

3. _____

The three things I know others like about me:

1. _____

2. _____

3. _____

Leadership Communication Self-Test

Skill Set	Evaluation			
	Always 5	Mostly 4	Not Enough 2	Almost Never 1
1. Do you understand your impact on people, and adjust your approach accordingly?				
2. Do you tailor your communication techniques based on your audience?				
3. Do you address pre-existing barriers before trying to forge ahead?				
4. Do you tell meaningful stories to provide clarity and context for change?				
5. Do you use visual techniques to illustrate important concepts?				
6. Do you practice *no surprises* by regularly forecasting and closing the loop?				

© MDA Consulting Group

Skill Set	Evaluation			
	Always 5	Mostly 4	Not Enough 2	Almost Never 1
7. Do you take the time to put important items down in writing to facilitate agreement?				
8. Do you intentionally choose language that accurately describes what you are thinking?				
9. Do you intentionally spread enthusiasm for the positive?				
10. Do you avoid getting defensive when challenged by colleagues and employees?				

Total Points: _____

Scoring

MASTER: 40 points or higher—You set an excellent example. You will improve your organization if you actively teach these skills to others.

ADVANCED: 30-39 points—You are better than most, and could be excellent if you seek out feedback from others and apply your learning.

INTERMEDIATE: 20-29 points—Your skills are under-developed. Be courageous, and look at every encounter as an opportunity to improve. Even the smallest changes will make a big difference.

About the Author

PAUL BATZ IS AN EXECUTIVE COACH, PROFESSIONAL SPEAKER AND COMMUNITY LEADER, with expertise in business development, influence and building the spirit of accountability into organizations. *Inspire, Persuade, Lead: Communication Secrets of Excellent Leaders* is his first book. Now in the third edition, the book is a teaching tool in corporate and university leadership programs. Paul also participated in *Conversations on Leadership*, a book project of 17 leaders published in 2004 by Insight Publishing. Paul is an owner and president of MDA Leadership Consulting—one of the fastest growing leadership consulting firms in the country. Clientele includes senior business leaders and strategic HR leaders in many prominent Fortune 100 and 500 growth companies. The firm is driven by the belief that *without great leadership, nothing works.*

On his 40th birthday, Paul was elected Chair of the Board for Lutheran Social Services of Minnesota—one of America's most influential non-profit social service organizations. As a former executive and partner with the national communications firm Padilla Speer Beardsley, his work has won awards in both the public relations and advertising industries. Audiences and coaching clients agree, his style is invigorating and his work is inspiring. For more information visit www.mdaleadership.com, or call 612.332.8182 for ideas on how you can improve your leadership influence with the people important to your success.